Praise for Paul Axtell and *Meetings Matter*

"Meetings can be a mind-numbing squandering of time, money, patience, and other finite resources. But they needn't—and shouldn't—be. In *Meetings Matter*, Paul Axtell shows how thoughtful, respectful, and focused conversation is the key to effective meetings. What's more, he provides lots of specific strategies and tactics. Adopt the practices suggested here and the meetings you attend will never be fruitless again. The bonus? You and your colleagues will be more engaged than ever in producing great results."

— Rodger Dean Duncan,
author of *Change-friendly Leadership*

"I have been following Paul's teaching in organizations for more than a decade now. The essence is: When people matter, things get done, and they get done in amazing ways!"

—Audie Penn, Master Black Belt, Caterpillar Production Systems Global Deployment, Caterpillar, Inc.

"This book should be called *Magical Meetings* because if you follow Axtell's advice, you will find magic—your meetings will not only be magically productive, they'll be fun!"

—Ernie Jaworski, National Academy of Sciences Distinguished Fellow

"This is a brilliant resource, written in an accessible style. I have no doubt it will be a treasured guidepost for leaders who desire to increase their effectiveness. Paul Axtell demonstrates that conversation is not only the key to effective groups, but also the foundational skill to building a quality life."

—Larry Roper, Vice Provost,
Oregon State University

"Paul Axtell's ideas around designing, leading, and participating in meetings produce immediate shifts in the ability to contribute to better meeting outcomes. Paul has a gift for boiling any skill down to the five to seven key ideas that are critical to keep in one's awareness. He communicates these ideas in a clear, concise fashion, which makes them easy to put to use."

—Lynda Rands, Executive Coach,
WorkLife Resources

"More and more work time is spent in meetings, but Paul Axtell's practical advice ensures that the time spent in those meetings is outcomes focused while enhancing the quality of relationships. Through my interactions with Paul, I have become a better person to be with and a better overall leader."

—Shari Mickey-Boggs, Associate Vice President and
Chief Human Resources Officer, Wright State University

"This is powerful stuff, and it is easy to see how it can be put to use to make almost everything I do on a daily basis better. It's a book every professional should read—it will not only make meetings more productive, but people more efficient, successful, and happier."

—Dwight Brimley, Finance Coordinator

"While this book provides an accessible path to great meetings, it is also rich with insights about interpersonal relationships, leadership, project management, and what constitutes a healthy, productive organization."

—Gwil Evans, Emeritus Professor of Communications,
Oregon State University

Meetings Matter

Meetings
Matter

Eight Powerful
Strategies for
Remarkable
Conversations

Paul Axtell

JACKSON CREEK PRESS • CORVALLIS, OREGON

Design by Cheryl McLean
Cover author photo by Cindy Officer

Other books by Paul Axtell:
Ten Powerful Things to Say to Your Kids
Being Remarkable

paulaxtell.com

JACKSON CREEK PRESS
2150 Northwest Jackson Creek Drive
Corvallis, Oregon 97330
info@jacksoncreekpress.com
541.752.4666 • fax 541.588.8434

ISBN 978-0-943097-14-5
Library of Congress Control Number: 2014950876

Printed in the United States of America

Contents

Foreword xi

Preface. xiii

Acknowledgments. xvii

Introduction 1

Strategy 1: Choose the Perspective: This Matters 13

Strategy 2: Master Effective Conversation 23

Strategy 3: Create Supportive Relationships 43

Strategy 4: Decide What Matters and Who Cares. 67

Strategy 5: Design Each Conversation 83

Strategy 6: Lead Meetings for Three Outcomes 119

Strategy 7: Participate in Meetings to Add Impact 165

Strategy 8: Build Remarkable Groups. 191

The Art of Learning to Be Effective 211

Guidelines for Managers 231

Dealing with Ineffective Behavior in Meetings 261

Appendix A: Tailored Designs 277

Appendix B: Relationship-Building Exercises 291

Appendix C: Assessment Tools. 301

Appendix D: Tools for Continued Exploration. 309

Bibliography 337

Index 341

About the Author 347

Foreword

Every now and again, a book crosses my desk that becomes beloved. Beloved for its cogent advice, its engaging style, and its tremendous ability to get to the heart of a business problem that is driving us collectively crazy. *Meetings Matter* is such a book.

Unleashing Paul Axtell's genius at running and organizing effective meetings, this book provides ideas for each of us and all of us to be better…better with our coworkers, better for our organizations, and better human beings. Paul says his hope is that the book will become dog-eared from frequent use, and I am among those who firmly believe that it will.

Paul's expertise has been earned through experiences and observation, values and insights, all harvested and honed in a life's journey that took him inside workplaces of all kinds. The commonality of these is the recognition that people are at the heart of every organization, and harnessing their talent through conversations and relationships in a respectful, engaging, and purposeful way is not only good for business, it is good for people.

I met Paul when he came to my large research university in the late 1990s as we were striving to become a greater place, not only for ourselves, but to better serve the public that entrusted us with its resources. With the turnover of leadership, the changing expectations of elected officials and donors, and the inevitable "new ideas" from faculty, staff, and students, we often found ourselves in turbulent "white water." We were navigating those early years of the changing ecosystem of higher education, which translated to a lot of activity and excitement without enough to show for it except being dripping wet. While I had nothing to do with bringing Paul to that wonderful campus, I have forever been changed by his insights, patience, gentle toughness, and clarity of thought, and the campus found a way to unify around a new and strategic direction that has led to impressive success over the past fifteen years.

Paul helped me understand more deeply the importance and power of bringing a productive perspective into a conversation, of listening, of preparing before and following up after meetings. These skills improved my focus on outcomes and the next steps we needed to get there. Paul is clear on the vitally important notions of completion, clarity, candor, and commitment, and of being thoughtful and taking care of the ideas as well as the people in the conversation.

Above all, Paul's constant emphasis on the importance and value of being genuine is apparent on every page. What a gift. Despite our best efforts—and speaking from personal experience—from time to time we do come unprepared to a meeting, make mistakes of substance or style, get off track, or use humor to lighten the moment and in so doing marginalize a participant. *Meetings Matter* gives permission, if you will, to make errors and then learn from them, recover relationships and ideas hurt by them, and come effectively back to the tasks at hand.

I highly recommend *Meetings Matter*, whether your chair in the executive seat is well worn or you are just beginning your career. This book is a manual for meetings that is well organized, coherent, and offers proven ideas and clarity on the core concepts. Appropriate for everyone who has organized or attended a meeting, this book has earned its place on my recommended list . . . and is within easy reach on my closest bookshelf.

—*Timothy P. White*
Chancellor, California State University

Preface

I'm writing this book for you . . . the manager who recognizes that meetings are at the core of the work you do, the supervisor who understands that people matter, the employee who wants to contribute as much as possible, the project leader who wants every team meeting to add velocity to the project.

My hope is that you will find ideas that resonate with your experience and that you will delight in applying them immediately in your meetings. And even better, that you will find yourself thinking about and applying many of the ideas to your life away from work. Work is important, but family and friends matter more.

Two things I care about—the result of being trained as a chemical engineer—are reflected throughout this book. First, I love process and seeing the impact of working with critical variables in any discipline. Second, I have a keen interest in and respect for people who, like myself, dedicated themselves to technical fields only to realize they somehow missed out on interpersonal skills. While this book might not have you dancing at parties, it just might give you what you need to feel much more comfortable in a world that swirls in conversations and relationships.

The inspiration

This collection of ideas began to form when, as a young engineer, I started teaching a course on problem solving and decision making. That beginning led to a thirty-year journey working to master designing conversations and leading meetings.

Still today, as I teach programs on individual and group effectiveness, participants have two primary areas of interest: how to improve their family relationships, and how to make their meetings more effective.

While nearly everyone who is asked will tell you they hate meetings, I don't think that's the case at all. I think people simply get frustrated wasting valuable time they could spend more productively elsewhere.

This book allows you to turn that around. It gives you a host of actions you can take to make that next meeting on your calendar a different experience. The ideas also have application beyond meetings. For example:

- Sometimes what's needed is a change of perspective. As human beings, we have the ability to change our mindset about aspects of life that we are not currently looking forward to.

- Putting time and attention toward creating and enhancing relationships is necessary for building our networks, and also for raising children, deepening friendships, and enjoying life.

- The way we listen and the way we speak—our conversations— are at the heart of understanding each other, having influence, and being effective both at work and at home.

- Awareness begins the process of learning. Once we identify the variables we need to pay attention to, whether it's while playing golf or when leading a meeting, we have access to getting better.

The bottom line is that your quest to improve your meetings will make a difference elsewhere in your life.

These ideas work

Twenty years ago, I trained a young supervisor named Audie. Every once in a while, I'd hear from him, either to let me know he had changed companies or to ask a question about some idea we had worked on in the initial training. Everywhere he went, he would put some of these ideas to work in his new organization.

Last year, Audie called and said he was working as a continuous improvement consultant for three of eleven plants in an organization. Senior management saw that those three plants were outperforming the other plants and embracing improvement practices more powerfully. When asked about the difference, Audie told them he had put together a plant-wide training program based on what he had learned twenty years ago.

The point is—the ideas in this book work. They are not difficult. You can trust the ideas and trust yourself in working with them. They are obvious, simple, and straightforward. They are simply the common sense that isn't very common.

A dog-eared guide

This is my dream for this book: That it ends up being dog-eared from use. That it sits close at hand on your desk or is kept ready in your briefcase or backpack. That you delve into it before meetings to help you plan and after meetings for reflection and refinement. That you refer to it when you are mentoring someone about working in a group setting. I sincerely hope you will wear out this book.

I would love to hear from you when you put an idea into practice. You'll find my contact information on my website, paulaxtell.com.

—*Paul Axtell*

"Everything changed the day
I figured out there was
exactly enough time
for the important things
in my life."

—Brian Andreas
American artist

Acknowledgments

There are three people without whom this book would not have happened. Gwil Evans was the first client who embraced the idea of designing meetings not only for outcomes, but also to change the experience of meetings for the participants. Gwil and I spent countless hours designing important retreats, budget meetings, and difficult-to-discuss topics. Cheryl McLean is a jack-of-all-trades editor who saw the possibility of a book that would be both useful and readable. Scott Adams, creator of the *Dilbert* comic strip, once said that goals don't make things happen—systems do, and Cheryl is a system that makes things happen. Lastly, Cindy, my wife, has been helping me refine the ideas and my training programs for a very long time. We have debriefed more days of training and meetings than we can remember.

In addition, Lynda Rands and Tom Scheuermann have worked with the chapters in this book from the beginning, providing questions and clarity that allowed me to rethink and reengage with writing that didn't quite capture ideas in the best way.

From an idea point of view, I owe a great deal to Tim Gallwey, Michael Nichols, Dale Carnegie, and countless other authors and teachers who contributed to my thinking on individual and group effectiveness. You will find their works listed in the bibliography and their teaching reflected throughout this book.

Since most of these ideas were refined while working, I'm indebted to the clients who trusted me with their people over the years and put the ideas into practice so they could be tested and refined.

I appreciate the advice and counsel of each of the following people: Cathy Baird, Todd Baker, Mike Bamberger, Paul Biwan, Cheri Boline, Linda Brewer, Dwight Brimley, Helen Brittain, Jessica Budge, Jayson Clairmont, Bill Cook, Michele Corkery, Dave Davis, Kathy Debellis, Jane Demmer, Dave DeVault, Thayne Dutson, Kristen Duus, Marek Eaton, Abbey Eisenhauer, Gwil Evans, Joe Fons, Cheryl Forlines, Lynn Friesth, Don Gallagher, Paul Garcia, Lucy Gardner, Paul Gibson, Lori Glander, Jill Handley, Barbara Henricks, Brian Henson, Jonathan Herman, Peg Herring, Charles Hura, Ernie Jaworski, Ron Jeitz, Keith Jeskey, Steve Johnson, Vickie Keith, Margaret Kingsbury, Hugh Kuehl, Sarah Lewis, Christiane Loehr, John Mann, Denise Mineck, Ricardo Molano, Todd Nell, Amy Nimmer, Chris Officer, Jack Ogami, Fariborz Pakseresht, Audie Penn, Larry Roper, Gary D. Smith, Keith Smith, Mary L. Smith, Alice Sperling, Jed Stafford, Ashlee Tate, Howard Templeton, Jim Thorne, Marilyn Trefz, Elizabeth Webb, Aaron Wetzel, Tim White, and Debra Wilcox. I am indebted to each of them.

"What we pay attention to,
and how we pay attention, determines
the content and quality of life."

—Mihaly Csikszentmihalyi
Hungarian psychologist

" If I look at my schedule and there aren't any meetings lined up, I immediately get some scheduled. Meetings are the work of the organization, and if I'm not meeting, I'm not moving things forward. "

—Amy Nimmer
Fortune 100 company executive

Introduction

What people are saying about meetings

> *"I can't wait to get out of here and get back to work!"*
>
> *"I didn't agree with what was being said, but we were already running way behind, so I didn't say anything."*
>
> *"No one is willing to bring up the real issues that need to be addressed."*
>
> *"Another meeting with no agenda."*
>
> *"We just talk about the same things over and over again— nothing ever gets done."*

People are concerned with the amount of time they spend in meetings —and the lack of accomplishment that occurs—for good reason.

People cherish time to focus on their commitments and projects. They take pride in being productive, and being in a meeting that is not productive is disheartening. And many people end up taking work home, which takes time away from their family, friends, and personal interests.

When people are in meetings, they want to contribute, and when a meeting isn't conducted in a way that allows them to do so, they leave feeling they had something to offer but couldn't. They expect supervisors, managers, and project leaders to know how to lead meetings, and when those expectations are unfulfilled, it can be frustrating and disappointing.

A colleague and I were walking, catching up on each other's lives. Donnie is a purchasing negotiations consultant, and I asked if he had any interesting ideas about meetings. His response was immediate and passionate: "I hate meetings. Think of all the talent and time that you have tied up in a meeting with ten people!"

His point is a good one. If a meeting isn't accomplishing specific goals or moving toward strategic outcomes, then that time and talent and the resources they represent are wasted. Meetings offer so much potential to move key initiatives and projects forward, it's disappointing when they don't. The organization pays a price when meetings are not effective, and every individual in the organization pays that price.

While Donnie's experience with meetings was clearly negative, the ideas in this book will create the possibility that it doesn't have to be that way. The talent in the room can be focused and energized— creating solutions, generating ideas, identifying opportunities, and moving with velocity toward accomplishing goals.

People don't hate meetings—they are simply frustrated because they're being kept from being as productive and remarkable as they could be.

We all want the same thing. Ask the people in your organization who lead meetings to list the seven things they wish were true about meetings that are not true now. Then ask people who attend meetings the same question. The lists will be almost identical.

We don't need to convince anyone that meetings should be different. We just need to identify the key strategies for improving them and then get started.

You will find three threads woven together throughout the book:

1. Meetings are important and are worthy of mastery.

2. Conversation and relationship provide the foundation not only for meetings, but for life.

3. Groups that can work together in a remarkable way create leverage and momentum.

Meetings matter and are worthy of mastery

"It took me fifteen years to make it look easy."
—Fred Astaire, American dancer

Meetings are at the heart of an effective organization, and each meeting is an opportunity to clarify issues, set new directions, sharpen focus, create alignment, and move objectives forward. With that kind of leverage at stake, it's imperative that we master the art of designing and leading meetings.

I've always loved activities that are tough to master: bridge, golf, fly fishing, dancing—tough to master and yet enjoyable soon after you take them up.

You can think about designing and leading meetings in the same way. Mastery might take fifteen years, as Fred Astaire suggests, yet it's easy to begin with a few ideas to implement and practice. You will immediately see progress.

The way to start is straightforward. Choose something to look for in every meeting. For example, consider these possibilities:

- Listen for the moment when a conversation goes off track, and then gently guide it back to the subject at hand.

- Look for who is indicating they would like to get into the conversation, and invite them in.

- Notice when someone interrupts: what happens to the conversation and to the person who was interrupted.

- Listen for when clarity is missing, and ask a question that causes clarity to emerge.

- Pay attention to whether specific actions are agreed upon after a discussion.

When you notice something that isn't working or that is missing, in that moment, you can choose to do something different. Awareness creates the opportunity for different responses—the choice to say or do something else—and therein lies the power of noticing.

Meetings are, in essence, a series of conversations, and effective conversation is like a puzzle with all the pieces in place. Improving your meetings by improving your conversations is not mysterious, but the impact can be dramatic.

One way to improve conversation is to look for the missing piece and provide it. This book will identify the ideas that are most likely to be missing and give you clear pathways toward mastering meetings.

Conversation and relationship provide the foundation

Conversation and relationship create the foundation not only for meetings, but also for everyday life. Almost every conversation can be enhanced, and when we make our conversations richer, our relationships go to another level of trust and openness and enjoyment.

My grandmother, Esther, had one request each Christmas—that for two hours at some time during the holidays, everyone would be in the same room talking. No games, television, or distractions were allowed. Only one person could speak at a time, and the youngest person got to start. After that person finished, he or she would pick the next person to speak. Sure, people got excited and jumped in from time to time, but for the most part the conversation flowed as intended. Those were conversations everyone in the family remembers fondly, even though it took the iron will of my grandmother to make them happen.

Can you describe a conversation that seems magical? It might feel like a wonderful exchange with a few friends—perhaps over coffee in the living room. It's the time when you are immersed in the conversation. People are speaking in a personal way that holds your attention. Everyone else is listening with no outward urgency about speaking. There is no apparent judging, just thoughtful consideration of what is being said, so each conversation is completed and each person feels heard. There isn't a right answer and there's no particular place to get to—no place other than right here, right now. And yet everyone leaves with something—clarity, new thinking, awareness, fulfillment, connection.

At this point, you are likely saying, "Sure, but I work in large groups, and we don't have time for the kind of conversation you are describing—nor do I think we could pull it off if we tried."

That's what this book is about—getting twenty people in a meeting to feel like five friends having a conversation over coffee. This is challenging, but possible.

Expect to be disappointed at the outset if you raise your standards for meetings. This is actually good news. It means you have created a gap in your awareness between where you are and where you want to be. Just treat it as an empowering gap—as an opportunity created for doing something more effectively.

Groups that can work together in a remarkable way create leverage and momentum

"The power of a group could be compared to a laser. Ordinary light is called 'incoherent,' which means that it is going in all kinds of directions; the light waves are not in phase with each other so they can't build up. But a laser produces a very intense beam which is coherent and can do all sorts of things that ordinary light can not."

— David Bohm, American theoretical physicist

Why are we talking about groups in a book on meetings? For two reasons. First, most meetings involve the same group of people coming together on a regular basis, and if they create a sense of unity, the conversation and results can get to beyond good. Second, we rely heavily on teams or task forces to take on initiatives and projects, and because of this, the quality of meetings is crucial.

I love the way Oregon State University Vice Provost Larry Roper put it: *Think about what could happen if people who care got together and talked about things that matter in a thoughtful, respectful way.*

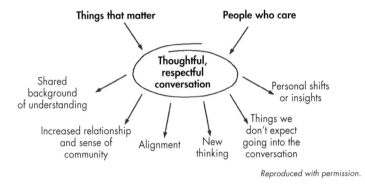

Reproduced with permission.

Educator and leadership consultant Judy Brown describes collective wisdom as thinking that emerges which no one had when they walked into the room. When groups work together in a remarkable way, individuals get new thinking, insights, and perspectives, and collectively the group's understanding deepens. Alignment occurs more quickly, and members readily take on work.

Perhaps the most important outcome is realizing the possibility of being a group that can talk about anything and everything that matters to the organization. If you can talk about anything, the power of a group, as David Bohm describes, becomes available. Imagine what a committed, cohesive group might accomplish.

Can we talk?

Maybe it's this simple: If we learn to trust ourselves
and the other person and the conversation,
it will almost always turn out.

What are the conversations we need to have together?

Navigating toward mastery: How to use this book

Rule number one: Turn your curiosity loose. Bounce around. Start anywhere you like. Like a field guide to birds, this is meant to be a reference you can access from almost any point. If you don't feel good about how you contribute to a meeting, go to strategy 7 on participating. If you want to do a better job of keeping your meetings on track, go to strategy 6 on leading. Follow your current needs and interests. Don't miss the "TRY THIS" boxes, which offer actions you can take to start putting these ideas to work.

While each section has been written to stand alone in support of your self-defined journey through the material, it's useful to have a sense of the overall book. The essence of the work on meetings is contained in strategies 4 through 7 on designing, leading, and participating in meetings, but the book doesn't start there because I feel strongly that without the first three strategies—perspective, conversation, and relationship—we simply will not get to where we want to be in our meetings.

- **Strategy 1. Choose the Perspective: This Matters.** Whenever we choose to treat something as though it matters, we give ourselves the opportunity to be remarkable. In a broader sense, our perspective on life and certainly on meetings determines how things work out. Effective people find empowering perspectives to shape their thinking and actions.

- **Strategy 2. Master Effective Conversation.** Conversation is central to being effective. Since meetings are essentially a series of conversations, the ability to speak, listen, and engage in thoughtful dialogue is required.

- **Strategy 3. Create Supportive Relationships.** Use meetings to build your network. Learn to work the room. Your ability to work together is determined by the amount of relationship that exists.

- **Strategy 4. Decide What Matters and Who Cares.** Put fewer things on the agenda. Invite fewer people. What is it that you should be discussing? Who must be there to do thorough work?

- **Strategy 5. Design Each Conversation.** The number one problem for most meetings is the lack of a clear and visible set of process steps to follow for each conversation. Six conversational designs will cover most topics.

- **Strategy 6. Lead Meetings for Three Outcomes.** Producing results takes first priority. Balancing participation for alignment and engagement is the second objective. Enhancing individual and organizational competence with meetings is the third outcome.

- **Strategy 7. Participate in Meetings to Add Impact.** Choose to "own" every meeting you attend. Always be looking for what will add value not only to the meeting, but to other participants. Be a player, not a spectator.

- **Strategy 8. Build Remarkable Groups.** Getting to know one another in a more profound way will result in better meetings and stronger groups. Remarkable groups can dream bigger, produce more, and influence productivity throughout the organization.

Three additional chapters add depth and answer questions that are not fully addressed elsewhere. Four appendixes offer more tools and resources for continued exploration.

- **The Art of Learning to Be Effective.** We've all attended training programs or read books and been excited about the ideas only to have them disappear. The current thinking about learning has shifted to awareness, insight, critical variables, and deliberate practice. This chapter shows how these ideas apply wherever you want to improve performance.

- **Guidelines for Managers.** Employees want to be connected to management, and they want to have a voice—adding ideas, expressing concerns, and being appreciated. The best way to make this happen is through conversation with their supervisors or managers. Engaging employees through conversation is at the heart of being a supervisor.

- **Dealing with Ineffective Behavior in Meetings.** This chapter provides options for dealing with some of the most common issues that arise in meetings, from people who hijack every conversation to someone whose negative perspective and comments derail the work of the group.
- **The appendixes** add a range of tools for designing meetings, building relationships, making assessments of where you are in terms of where you want to be, and giving you additional ways to put these ideas into practice. You will find more resources on the website at paulaxtell.com.

Rule number two: When in doubt, go back to rule number one and trust your instincts, follow your interests.

Get started

Meetings are plentiful. There is no need to read the book from start to finish or implement every idea all at once.

One of my favorite stories is from *Bird by Bird*, a book on writing by American novelist Anne Lamott. It applies to many aspects of life, including how you can approach learning to master the art of meetings.

> *Thirty years ago my older brother, who was ten years old at the time, was trying to get a report on birds written that he'd had three months to write. It was due the next day. We were out at our family cabin in Bolinas, and he was at the kitchen table close to tears, surrounded by binder paper and pencils and unopened books on birds, immobilized by the hugeness*

of the task ahead. Then my father sat down beside him, put his arm around my brother's shoulder, and said, "Bird by bird, buddy. Just take it bird by bird."

Two of the best ideas for tackling life are **get started** and **take it one piece at a time**. We all have situations in our lives where we are avoiding taking action for whatever reason. Left too long, these places become a source of frustration and discouragement. Collectively, we seem to have drifted to this place with meetings, and perhaps it's time to start learning to do them differently.

Whether you are the manager who calls meetings, a project leader who runs team meetings, or someone who attends meetings as a participant, you will find action items throughout this book to help make your conversations—and therefore your meetings—more effective. Find one idea that resonates with your own experience and put it into practice. Once you have that idea working for you, find another. Just take it meeting by meeting, idea by idea.

The first thing to do is to start—then take it "bird by bird."

" The real voyage of discovery consists not in seeing new landscapes but in having new eyes. "

—Marcel Proust
French novelist

Choose the Perspective:
This Matters

Core ideas:

- Choose empowering perspectives.
- Perspectives shape your experience—of meetings, of relationships, of life.
  - Each person, each conversation, and each moment is what matters.
  - Catch yourself with a disempowering viewpoint.
  - Find a new mindset for meetings.

" The greatest discovery of my
generation is that a human being
can alter his life by
altering his attitudes. "

—William James
American philosopher

Choose empowering perspectives

Most of this book focuses on the techniques, practices, and ideas required to make your meetings better. Unfortunately, even the best tactics cannot overcome a disempowering perspective. Other words for *perspective* are *mindset* or *point of view*. Whatever you call it, your perspective shapes your attitude and how you deal with life. And it is something you have the power to change.

Minor league baseball manager Rob Johnson, in an interview for the *St. Louis Post-Dispatch*, was asked about what determines who makes it to the major leagues. He answered: "There are three things you can control—your work ethic, your preparation, and your attitude." The point is that in every field there are some who make it because their talent far outreaches everyone else's. But that's only a few. The rest make it based on the three things that are within your control.

Therefore, throughout the book, you will notice perspectives that, if chosen and embraced, will have far more impact on your meetings than even the best meeting practices.

We all operate with certain perspectives in place—values we learned from our parents, from our coaches or mentors, from friends, or from lines in movies or books that resonated with our thoughts about ourselves or about life. Such phrases remind us of who we want to be or how we want to think about and respond to life. These phrases are everywhere. Here are several that have stuck with me:

- From Adam Wainwright, St. Louis Cardinals pitcher: "You can fall into a trap of being mediocre. If you're OK with mediocre, then you'll be mediocre." What a wonderful reminder about not settling for less than our best!

- From Sonny, the hotel manager in the movie *The Best Exotic Marigold Hotel:* "Everything will be all right in the end. If it's not all right, it is not yet the end." This gives us some freedom around learning; we need to be on the path and trust that it will eventually work out.

- "We can sleep when we get back to Poland." This came from a travel article in which the author described workers from Poland who, while working in Italy, would not slow down and rest despite her urging them to take a break. I love it as a reminder to stay with something until it is finished.

I'm sure you have your own touchstones to remind you about who you want to be, what you value, and how you want to interact with the world. The first step on the journey toward effective meetings begins with choosing an empowering way to view the entire notion of meetings. With a wonderful perspective, you can then focus on the strategies and actions that will make the most difference.

Perspectives shape your experience— of meetings, of relationships, of life

Sometimes you need to lead with your attitude. You simply need to choose to step into the world with a perspective that is empowering. Think about it: Attitude affects how you relate to life. When you realize you can shift your attitude on demand by choosing an empowering perspective, it changes everything.

Each person, each conversation, and each moment are what really matters

This is perhaps the most powerful perspective for shaping a positive experience in many aspects of life and work. You may be familiar with Tolstoy's story "The Three Questions," part of his collection *What Men Live By*:

- Where is the most important place?
- When is the most important time?
- Who is the most important person?

The answers are, of course:

- Right here.
- Right now.
- The person you're with.

The point is to give your full attention to whatever you are doing and to whomever you are with right now—to remind yourself that this moment matters because it's where you are. Remind yourself to be mindful.

> *"If I'm not happy in this time and place,*
> *I'm not paying attention."*
>
> —Jodi Hills, American author

Catch yourself with a disempowering viewpoint

Sometimes the first step in getting to an empowering perspective is to notice when you are not looking forward to an experience. By noticing that you are not relating to something powerfully, you open the door to choosing a different perspective.

It's easy to slip into dealing with certain tasks or situations mindlessly. You are not a bad person if you have slipped into this mode—we all do it. In fact, realizing that you haven't been relating to something as though it matters is actually useful. If you have been going through life this way, there is a tremendous upside to beginning to treat what you do as if it matters. If you are present and attentive and engaged in the moment, those around you will notice. In a world of distraction, busyness, and multitasking, attention is often fleeting. The key is mindfulness—to be fully present and engaged.

Effective people also notice when they are not looking forward to something or have thoughts that are not supportive. Then they choose a different perspective. Here's an example. My wife, Cindy, and I were driving to South Dakota for my mother's funeral. On the way, we had this exchange:

> CINDY: Where are you about the next few days?
>
> PAUL: Well, I'm going to get through this.
>
> CINDY: Insufficient.
>
> PAUL: What do you mean?
>
> CINDY: You need a different perspective. Yes, you will be dealing with sadness and grief. And you need to remember who you are in this family. Your job for the next few days is to welcome people and invite them to tell you wonderful stories about your mother.
>
> PAUL: Got it.

Now think about it. I've still got to get through it, but am I a different person for people if I am looking to welcome them, to include them, to have them tell me stories about my mom? Absolutely! Without Cindy's request for me to change my perspective, I would have spent a lot of time walking outside by myself, because that's how I deal with being upset. She helped me to shift my perspective, which led to many wonderful conversations about my mother—and an opportunity to learn new things about her friends and her past that were never shared before.

Here's an example of how adding a new perspective quickly changes behavior. A research laboratory asked me to conduct some interpersonal skills training for their security guards, because they consistently received complaints from visitors about how they'd been treated by the guards. Before I designed the training, I sat down with the guards and asked them what they thought they needed. Their reactions were enlightening: "No one told us about the complaints!" and "What do they want us to be, receptionists or security guards?"

About twenty minutes later, one of the guards said, "We can welcome people. We don't need any training. Someone just needed to tell us that our job has two parts: provide security for the facility and make people feel like guests. We can do this."

Then someone else said, "I always hated being a bad guy anyway!"

Everyone agreed that security and welcoming made sense, and the complaints went to zero. If you change your perspective, you see the world differently and behavior follows.

> *"Elegance is an attitude."*
> —Longines advertising campaign

Find a new mindset for meetings

Some of the most troubling perspectives for meetings are ones we have drifted into over time without thinking about it. If you pay attention, you'll hear people expressing, almost without realizing it, a series of comments about meetings that create a disempowering perspective overall:

"We have too many meetings, and they are booked back-to-back."

"We rarely get through the agenda, and the meeting still runs long."

"If I can find a way to avoid a meeting, I don't attend."

As a result, the predominant mindset about meetings is negative, and that colors how people prepare and participate. The mind tends naturally to focus on the negative and look for evidence to support that assessment. This is often a self-fulfilling prophecy: what you look for is what you get.

The way forward begins with noticing when your current attitude will not get you to where you would like to be. The next step is to choose a more positive perspective.

Here are two perspectives that provide a sound starting point for meetings: First, **meetings do matter**—they are high-leverage events at the heart of effective organizations. Second, **choose ownership for each meeting you attend**.

On a recent visit to a corporate office building, I saw a series of images of employees with the phrase, "I own the moment." This single phrase captures two powerful ideas: being present and being responsible. Each of these ideas will have an impact if you apply them to meetings. For example, if everyone treated each meeting as if it were their own and walked in looking for what they might do to make it successful, then your meetings would experience a profound shift in effectiveness.

Consider the saying: *If it is worth doing, it is worth doing right.* This is a perspective about life that applies here. Meetings are worth doing right, so walk into them with an empowering perspective.

> *"If you don't like something, change it.*
> *If you can't change it, change your attitude."*
>
> —Maya Angelou, American poet

A final perspective: This shall be

One of the fundamental variables in whether your meetings improve is how determined you are that they actually do change.

I love the term *intention* when it means "this shall be." Intention is different from a New Year's resolution, which tends to be treated as a wish or desire—hoped for but quickly forgotten in the demands of daily life.

Knowing you want something is not the same as being intentional about making it happen. For example, if you asked me what mattered in raising my kids—sports or academics—I'd say it was always academics, no question. Still, when I came home every evening, what I said wasn't *Let's go read*; it was *Let's go play catch*. In other words, I gave up that which I knew to be important. I simply lacked the intention to make it happen.

You already know that meetings hold enormous potential for moving organizational priorities forward. This book shows you how to design, lead, and participate in meetings to make a difference. The question is, will you make it happen?

TRY THIS

☐ Practice doing one thing at a time. Focus all your attention on this particular situation in this moment. See what happens.

☐ Catch yourself not looking forward to something, then find a new perspective.

☐ Practice owning the meetings you attend, then be aware of what you notice and what you might do differently.

☐ Put together a collection of seven phrases that remind you of how you want to deal with life.

" Each person's life
is lived as a
series of conversations. "

—Deborah Tannen
American linguistics professor

Master Effective
Conversation

Core ideas:

- Conversation is at the heart of being effective.
- Listening is a fine art.
- Be responsible for how you speak.
- Clarity, candor, commitment, and completion are the keys to effective conversation.
- Conversation shapes your world.

"While no single conversation is guaranteed to change the trajectory of a career, a business, a marriage, or a life, any single conversation can."

—Susan Scott
Fierce Conversations

Conversation is at the heart of being effective

It's so easy to take something for granted until you don't have it, like breathing, until you suddenly can't catch your breath. Conversation is like that. Conversations are the threads that weave the fabric of our lives, yet we don't pay attention until they're unraveling.

This chapter is about slowing down, looking at the impact of conversation in the broadest sense, and exploring practices you can learn that will improve the quality of your conversations. The perspective that conversation matters is fundamental in getting to where we want to be with meetings. Why? First, because a meeting is in essence a series of conversations. Second, because conversation is how you create relationships, and it's easier to converse when you know and respect everyone in the meeting.

Although we've been speaking and listening our whole lives, we have not spent much time reflecting on or building competence with everyday conversations. It's a missing piece.

We work on specialized conversations—presentation skills, negotiating skills, sales approaches, conflict resolution. We have not focused on the everyday conversations that make up most of life—catching up with each other, exchanging commitments, showing appreciation, sharing concerns, making decisions.

We also haven't been students of how to work with others or how to be great with people by paying attention to how we converse with each other. Nor have we worked on the process skills that are key to conducting conversations in group settings.

2

CONVERSATION

In workshops on individual and group effectiveness, I ask people to consider that after mastering their core discipline of accounting or engineering, their next area of focus should be conversation: speaking, listening, social skills, and meeting skills—all of which are at the heart of being effective in an organization.

Consider that there is a way of listening that allows people to speak authentically, a way of speaking that engages and influences the thinking of others, and a way of managing the conversation that leads to higher levels of accomplishment.

Acknowledging that conversation is at the heart of what you do creates an awareness for what you say and how you say it, for how you listen, and for how you participate in conversations. Your ability to lead, to get things done, to exercise influence, and to nurture relationships lies within the world of conversation.

Making conversations work

If you embrace the importance of conversation, then you can focus on understanding and noticing what it takes to make every conversation work out as intended.

These are the fundamental practices for effective conversation:

- Listen in a way that encourages others to keep speaking.
- Be responsible for your speaking: be aware of what you say and how you say it.
- Notice when one of these aspects of an effective conversation is missing: clarity, candor, commitment, or completion.

Listening is a fine art

One of the most influential articles I've ever read was about listening. *Utne Reader* reprinted a chapter from American journalist Brenda Ueland's book, *Strength to Your Sword Arm*. The article was titled "Tell Me More" and described what magical things happen when someone is speaking in the presence of a person who knows how to listen without interruption or without changing the conversation— someone who can listen wholeheartedly and then, when needed, add the supportive request, *Tell me more.*

Of course, there are times when good conversation is a back-and-forth affair, even a bit chaotic. But underlying those conversations is the notion of being able to slow down and just listen. So often that's all people need—to be heard.

Years ago, I taught a program called "A Special Evening on Listening" for some of my corporate clients and their families. During the session, we did an exercise on listening in which the person listening could not say anything at all. It's actually an exercise in devoting your complete attention to the person who is speaking so he or she truly feels heard. We used topics like these:

> *Tell me about the neighborhood in which you grew up.*
>
> *What are some of your favorite memories?*
>
> *When you dream or think about the future, what is it like?*
>
> *Tell me about your friends and what you like about them.*
>
> *What do you lie awake at night worrying about?*

In the first two rounds, family members split up and worked with people they did not know. My intent was to get everyone comfortable with the listening process before they talked within their own families. Then parents and children had a chance to practice listening to each other. A couple of weeks later, I received an e-mail from Andrea, one of the participants:

> *Dear Paul,*
>
> *Last night my fourteen-year-old daughter, Chelsea, came home and said, "Mom, I need to talk. If you can listen to me the way we learned the other evening, you can save me a three-mile bicycle ride to my friend's house."*
>
> *Thank you,*
> *Andrea*

I loved that. What a difference it can make to simply *listen* in a different way. It's a skill to be practiced.

A wonderful book by Michael Nichols, *The Lost Art of Listening*, makes the point that people typically listen to comprehend or to follow along in a conversation rather than to participate nonverbally in a way that lets the person speaking know you "got" what they said. You may have heard the expression, "Got it," in movies. The earliest reference I recall was in the movie *The Court Jester* with Danny Kaye:

> *"Get it?"*
> *"Got it."*
> *"Good."*

That's what we're after. Nichols says that just listening without adding to or changing the conversation is what is important. **Reassuring someone isn't listening. Trying to solve the problem isn't listening. Just listening is listening.** And when people feel we are interested and paying attention, they will speak about the things that matter to them.

Yet we don't listen very often, at least not in a way that is magical. We interrupt. We finish other people's sentences. We pretend to listen. Sometimes we don't even pretend. And certainly, we don't often intend to make a difference with someone by listening to them.

We all have a natural ability to listen. What we're after is developing an uncommon ability. A student of the influential American psychologist Carl Rogers once remarked that Rogers listened so intently it was as if he were "even listening with his shoes!"

You listen in an uncommon way in situations where you realize you have nothing to offer but your attention—when there is nothing you can say that will help. That's when you listen in a profound way. With a little attention and practice, you can discover how to draw on this capability more often.

Listening shows interest and caring

Attention and *caring* are tightly connected. If you pay attention to someone who is speaking in a meeting or you pay attention to your small kids when they want to talk, they will interpret that you care.

On the other hand, if you walk into someone's office and the person sees you come in but keeps typing while you talk, you get the impression this person doesn't care or isn't interested in what you have to say.

Similarly, if the top person in a meeting brings other work or constantly checks a smartphone or engages in side conversations, other people in the meeting get the impression that their speaking or the conversation of the group is not important.

Pay attention to the quality of your listening

There are all kinds of reasons you might stop listening in a conversation, but the moment you notice, there's your opportunity to refocus and start listening again.

You can likely recall being with someone who, when you were speaking, seemed to put the rest of the world on hold and be mindful only of you. These moments are memorable because they don't happen very often, and they demonstrate what's important here: *The level of attention and the quality of the listening impact whether a conversation stays at a superficial level or deepens.*

Conversation can be characterized as a dance where speaking is always in step with listening. If you ask a great question and then pay attention and really listen to the answer, your partner in the conversation will almost always respond in a thoughtful, authentic way. Of course, at times the other person will want you to share your thinking, so notice when you are invited to do so.

Listening is the interpersonal skill that makes productive conversations possible. Listening is the gift that allows speaking. If you listen, wonderful things can happen: people feel supported, issues get clarified, people open up, ideas come forth, frustrations disappear, creativity emerges, and self-esteem soars.

TRY THIS

☐ For the next week, stop and devote your full attention to everyone who speaks to you.

☐ Allow people to finish without interruption.

☐ Be slower to offer solutions or advice.

Be responsible for how you speak

"The meaning of your communication
is the response it elicits."

—Gregory Bateson, English social scientist

If I ask you, *Are you responsible for what you say in life?* you will no doubt respond affirmatively. If I ask you, *Are you also responsible for how people take what you say?* you are likely to say no. And most people would agree with you.

Still, if you want to be better than good with people, consider this point of view: *You are responsible not only for what you say, but for how it is received.* No one expects this of you, but it is a perspective you can choose.

A key part of self-awareness is knowing how you come across to others. The more aware you are, the more chance you have of choosing to come across positively. From this point of view, it's useful after each meeting to reflect on your speaking. If you reflect on what you say and how you say it, you'll stimulate your awareness and trigger thinking about what you might work on to be more effective.

Here are some questions to help you develop a sense of your conversational style:

- *What conversations do people associate with you? What topics do you bring up consistently? In each of your relationships and in each of your teams, what conversations are you known for?*

- *What's it like to talk with you? How do people feel after speaking with you?*

- *What is the impact of your speaking on others? Does your speaking have a positive or a negative impact?*

2

CONVERSATION

We all can identify people whose manner of speaking gets in the way of good conversation—people who:

- hijack every conversation, turning it to themselves or their stories,
- are so opinionated we no longer like to be around them,
- speak more often or longer than people can tolerate,
- introduce negative conversations into the organization, or
- make discounting remarks about others.

Part of self-development is being aware of what you do, noticing and acknowledging what you've noticed—what works and what doesn't—then making a conscious choice about what you do next. The goal is to speak in a way that is authentic, respectful, easy to hear, relevant, and impactful.

Bottom line: *What is it like for others to be in conversation with you?*

Clarity, candor, commitment, and completion are the keys to effective conversation

Effective conversation has these four elements: clarity, candor, commitment, and completion. These are the important pieces of the puzzle called conversation. A conversation may seem fine, but then you later discover that the intended actions or the expected alignment does not occur. When a conversation does not have the desired result, one of these pieces is likely missing.

I love this simple and elegant model because it gives you four things to pay attention to in all conversations. Let's work through each of these elements, one at a time.

The four Cs of conversation

Clarity means everyone understands what is being said in the same way. When people leave conversations without clarity, they are forced to make interpretations about what happened or about what someone truly thinks. Or they leave thinking one thing and others leave thinking something else.

Candor means everyone says what they think. It means being authentic, honest, and straightforward. It's not about saying anything and everything that occurs to you. It's about being willing to express what hasn't yet been said that would add value or would let people know where you stand on an issue. Without candor, you sacrifice ideas and alignment.

Commitment means you agree on who will take what actions and in what time frame after the conversation. Without specific commitments in time, you shouldn't expect anything to happen. Discussing an item does not mean anyone will do anything about it. It's simply good project management to determine who will do what by when.

Completion means everything that needs to be said or asked has been expressed before moving on to the next topic. If things are left unsaid or questions are not asked, you can't expect that people are either clear or aligned.

Check for clarity

> *"The problem with communication is the illusion that it has occurred."*
>
> —Sigmund Freud, Austrian neurologist

As Freud suggests, it might not be obvious when clarity is missing in a conversation. Lack of clarity is responsible for many avoidable misunderstandings and mistakes.

2
CONVERSATION

Clarity is often missing for a number of reasons. General terms and language leave people thinking they understand what someone means when they may not. Or people may feel uncomfortable questioning someone else, especially if the other person is higher in the organization or doesn't welcome being challenged. Or when a meeting is running behind, people often leave questions unanswered rather than cause further delay.

But clarity is too important to sacrifice for expediency or comfort. Here's why:

- It is easier to start a project if you are clear about how to start.

- It is easier to respond to a complaint if you are clear about what happened.

- It is easier to align if you know exactly what is being proposed.

- It is easier to fulfill requests and expectations if they are specific.

- There is less danger of things going awry after the meeting if you stay in each conversation until everyone understands it in the same way.

One of the final agenda items at many management retreats is agreeing on how everyone will answer the question: "What happened at the retreat?" During the meeting, each conversation seemed clear. Everyone thought they understood what was decided or where the conversation ended, but now they are not so sure. This final check surfaces any differences in how people interpret or remember what occurred during the retreat and provides clarity going forward.

TRY THIS

☐ In your meetings for the next week, observe conversations for clarity.

☐ Whenever you notice yourself wondering what someone else means, ask for clarity.

Speak with candor

"I find that if I say what I'm really thinking and feeling, people are more likely to say what they really think and feel. The conversation becomes a real conversation."

—Carol Gilligan, American psychologist

Candid conversation is at the heart of effective conversation. Candor means being authentic—saying what you mean and meaning what you say—speaking straight.

This is a cornerstone of groups that work well together. It's part of relationships that are special. Life is difficult enough without wondering about what your colleagues or friends really think.

The importance of candor is also one reason for keeping your working groups as small as possible. It's easier to be candid—to push back on each other, to be direct, to ask people what they think—with groups of only four or five. It's not impossible to get there with twenty or thirty people, but it requires time spent getting to know each other and an explicit agreement to be candid.

How might you get candor to be the norm in your meetings? First, be a role model in saying what you think when it is appropriate and adds value to the conversation. Next, continually look for opportunities to invite other people to share their thoughts. Master these two questions, which are designed to elicit ideas, concerns, and questions as well as personal views and where people stand on an issue:

"What do you think?"

"Where are you on this?"

Candor and civility—a dilemma

Candor is saying what you think and feel in a way that can be understood—in a way that is clear. There are lots of reasons people are not candid, perhaps driven by the desire to be comfortable combined with the fear of making others uncomfortable.

On the other hand, people who are passionate about creativity and collaboration argue that we've lost our edge in creativity by being overly concerned with being civil.

Perhaps it's not an "either/or" situation. Perhaps it's a "both/and" situation. Using a respectful tone of voice and setting up comments to establish a context of good intentions can allow you to say what you need to say in a way that can be heard.

This is a place where intention matters. If you begin your comments with the intention to be supportive and caring as well as straightforward and candid, you will be.

Ask for commitments

Commitment is a powerful word in two contexts. The first is in terms of what you care about—you are committed to your family, your friends, your faith, your community, and your dreams.

The second context is in terms of the next two or three weeks. This is the time period that effective people focus on to determine what they want to accomplish. If you commit to completing something by a certain date, it is much more likely to happen than if it is simply added to your list of things to do.

Most people are more productive when facing deadlines. If you study project management, you will see an emphasis on outcomes, time lines, milestones, and specific actions. If you are specific when you ask someone to do something, and if you ask for it to be done by a certain date, it is more likely to happen.

Still, people don't ask for this kind of specific commitment because they think it might be interpreted as micromanaging or a lack of trust. In cultures, organizations, or families where indirectness is the predominant pattern, requesting this level of specificity can be seen as confronting.

The question is, would the achievement of your project or goals be enhanced with specific commitments in time? Since the answer is most likely yes, then ask for commitments with due dates.

One of the keys to project management is to have commitments be specific with respect to *what* will be done, *when* it will be done, and *who* will do it. You're asking for someone to do something (X) by a specific time (Y) and, if something gets in the way of fulfilling that commitment, to agree in advance to pick up the phone and call you. I refer to this kind of commitment as "X by Y or call."

It sounds simple, but this can be tough. You are likely to encounter some resistance from people who think it is not necessary to be so specific. Well, lots of things in life are tough to implement, but that's why they make so much difference when you do.

Check for completion

This means not leaving a conversation until all parties are ready to end the discussion. While this is a simple courtesy, it also ensures that no critical point or question is left unexpressed.

Among the ways you might check for completion are these:

"What else would anyone like to add or ask about this?"

"Are there any lingering questions about this?"

"I'm ready to change topics; are you good with where we are?"

Conversation shapes your world

"Language is very powerful. Language does not just describe reality. Language creates the reality it describes."

—Desmond Tutu, South African cleric

Conversations shape who we are. They shape our experience of life. We make decisions about what is possible for ourselves early in life, and most people can identify decisions they made about themselves based on what they were told or what was said in their presence.

A conversation Cindy and I overheard at a baseball game in St. Louis illustrates a key idea about the impact of conversation. Right in front of us was a family of three: a girl, about five, her brother, about seven, and their dad. The girl had a baseball hat and glove, and she sat on the edge of her seat hoping for a foul ball. Whenever one came close, she would leap up and yell, "Get it for me, Daddy!"

About the fourth inning, this conversation occurred:

GIRL: Daddy, can girls play in the major leagues?

DAD: Nope, they're not allowed.

GIRL: Why not?

BOY: 'Cause if they get hit by a ball they'll cry.

The conversation ended at this point, and Cindy and I were left wondering if the father even realized what had just taken place—the limited future created for his daughter with this conversation. We were reminded once more about the impact of language: ***Words and conversations shape how we think about ourselves and the world.***

In my case, the conversation was about being shy. As a child, when guests arrived and were introduced, I wouldn't say anything. My mother, being supportive, would step in and cover for me. "Oh, just give him a little time; he's just shy." At my first grade teacher's conference with Ms. Jenner, the same exchange occurred. Ms. Jenner commented on my lack of participation in class, and my mother explained that I was just shy. When you are young, you begin to think of yourself in the ways people describe you and act in a way that is consistent with those labels or stories. Shyness is a particularly limiting story. I'd love to do high school over—I'd have a date this time. It was also hard to contribute early on in my career because I tended not to participate or speak.

A client, Larry Roper, tells the story of a conversation he had with his mother when he was in college, and her words have guided him for decades in determining where he spends his time and energy:

*"You are either going to wear out or rust out in life.
I suggest you wear out doing something
that is good for your soul."*
—Claudette Roper

You can most likely recall a time when someone had a conversation with you—a boss, a parent, a friend—a conversation you still remember, one that helped determine who you are today.

Conversations also shape the culture in which we live and work. One of my favorite sayings is, *If you want to change your kids, change their playgrounds and their friends.* In other words, put your kids into a different set of conversations.

Similarly, the mood in an organization is heavily influenced by the conversations that take place in it. What conversations take place around you? How do these conversations define the organization? Are they moving the organization forward or getting in the way?

You have something to say about each and every conversation in which you participate—and therefore with every person you touch each day. *What are the conversations you want to work and live within?*

Bottom line: *Conversation matters.* Although everyone grows up knowing the basics of how to speak and listen, day in and day out most people simply don't think about their conversations. And, like most things in life, when you stop being mindful of what you are doing or saying, you lose your ability to be more effective in the moment.

2
CONVERSATION

TRY THIS

☐ After each meeting, reflect on what you said and how you said it, taking note of your observations or insights.

☐ As each meeting topic is wrapped up, assess it against the four elements of effective conversation: clarity, candor, commitment, and completion. Speak up if anything is missing that would be useful to add.

☐ Look for examples of how words shape the world for you and others.

"Each conversation we have with our coworkers, customers, significant others, and children either enhances those relationships, flatlines them, or takes them down. Given this, what words or level of attention do you wish to bring to your conversations with the people most important to you?"

—Susan Scott
Fierce Conversations

"The real organization is always a dense network of relationships."

—Margaret J. Wheatley
American author

Create
Supportive
Relationships

Core ideas:

- Everything gets easier with good relationships.
- Building relationships is part of the job.
- Conversation creates relationship.
  - Don't wait for team building.
- Use your meetings to build your network.
  - Learn to work the room in meetings.
  - Overcome common connection hurdles.
- Without attention, relationships decline.
  - Checking in with people is a lost art.
  - Develop a system for keeping track of your relationships.

 The conversation is
the relationship.

—David Whyte
English poet

Everything gets easier with good relationships

American business writer Tom Peters once said, "Relationships are all you have." This serves as a wonderful reminder that relationships have tremendous influence in our lives—including in our meetings.

At work, relationships shape our ability to get things done, and the effectiveness of any meeting is shaped by the degree of relationship that exists among the people who walk into the room. One-on-one meetings with a close friend or someone you trust and respect are effortless. Meetings with four or five colleagues who like each other are also easy. Why? You have a level of relationship that allows you to talk freely. Larger meetings get exponentially more difficult because the level of relationship among group members is often not consistent with authentic, candid conversation.

Certainly, thoughtful meeting design and masterful leading can overcome limitations in relationships, especially if people walk in prepared to be open-minded, respectful, and ready to give others the benefit of the doubt. Still, having good relationships makes everything easier.

Can you design and conduct meetings so that the conversations you have in the meetings build and strengthen your relationships? Yes! Everything in this book is written with this in mind.

In fact, your meetings can be a primary place to build and enhance your network of relationships—the relationships that will allow you to be successful not only in meetings, but with every aspect of your work in the organization.

This strategy is important to me because meeting people and building relationships didn't come easily, and it's certainly not my preference in life. Still, you and I can be very good at things that don't align with our personal preferences or desire for comfort. This is one area where it is worthwhile to step out of your comfort zone.

Building relationships is part of the job

With today's hurry-up pace, it seems we've simply lost the notion of slowing down and taking time to be interested in other people. Front porches have been replaced with fenced-in backyards. Company softball teams have disappeared. Events designed to get employees together after work no longer hold the same interest. We've lost track of what is happening in other people's lives. We eat at our desks, and there doesn't seem to be time to go out for coffee.

Let's make time. There is something about the invitation to have coffee that carries a genuine interest in the other person, in connecting. Sure, Facebook and LinkedIn are designed for keeping in touch with the people in your personal and work lives to some extent. But nothing beats face-to-face conversations for developing a sense of connection and understanding. And those connections forged over coffee, tea, or lunch can provide value beyond getting to know one another better— they affect your ability to get things done in the organization.

During a leadership seminar, Ashlee shared a couple of her favorite insights about being in a leadership role. I loved this one, which she called: "With whom do I need to have a cup of coffee?"

As we were in the beginning of a new product launch, Mary Pat and I were feeling the pressure: a lot to do, and a short time to do it. It was chaotic. During a rough moment, Mary Pat said, "I am failing. I feel as if I am failing."

"Why?" I asked her. "All launches are chaos, and we just need to get through it."

She then said to me, "When Dave had this job, it wasn't this chaotic. He would be having a cup of coffee with someone now instead of being out here on the factory floor."

I looked at her as if she were nuts and asked how a cup of coffee would make things less chaotic. She said, "Dave knew when and with whom he needed to be building relationships to avoid the chaos and indecision."

Her statement has stuck with me for years. I now evaluate situations and question where a cup of coffee could solve my problem, or at a minimum make it less painful.

For many reasons, projects stop moving or commitments are not kept. If you have a relationship in place with the folks involved, discussing the problem is much easier. It's tough to bring up an issue with someone you don't know. Over coffee might just be the best way to have difficult conversations.

There is something about disengaging from the hectic pace of work and life—stepping away, slowing down—that creates an environment of calm and safety and permission. It allows for conversations about things that matter. And I'm not talking about a huge time investment here. Thirty minutes, once a week, and you could make new connections or deepen your relationship with fifty colleagues in a year's time.

Take Ashlee's advice and begin your day by thinking of someone you might invite to coffee.

If you are working globally, then rather than going out for coffee, set up some one-on-one phone calls simply to chat and catch up on life. And when you are in the same city, make time for learning more about the other person's story.

Conversation creates relationship

Groups can build a sense of relationship and trust by having productive, thoughtful conversations as they work together, but there is a definite advantage to getting to know one another first.

When working with a group of people who see the potential to operate at a higher level together, my focus is on three things:

- How can I improve their ability to talk with one another?
- How can our work together lead to more connection and trust within the group?
- What do they need to talk about?

Spending time getting to know one another in new ways increases the safety, authenticity, and quality of their conversations.

A client once called to ask if I would come and do a team-building day with his factory leadership team and the union representatives. Both sides were eager to begin making progress on issues they needed to resolve. Both sides thought the problem was a matter of trusting each other. My schedule precluded doing it within three months, so I offered a way for them to get started without me. I simply gave them a listening exercise to begin each of their weekly meetings.

The exercise consisted of three rounds of one-on-one listening, each round with a new partner. One person spoke to a question for three minutes while the other person just listened without asking questions or making comments. Then they exchanged roles for another three minutes. At the end of the round, they found new partners and spoke about a different question.

The total exercise took eighteen minutes at the beginning of each three-hour meeting. One week a union representative would choose the three questions to be used. The next week a member of the management team would bring three questions. (This exercise and a list of questions can be found in appendix B, pages 292–295.)

The rest of the story: When my schedule opened up, they no longer needed me. Getting to know one another was enough to change how they spoke and listened to each other. For me, this experience confirmed that if you can get people to share about the things in life that matter to them, you create a level of relationship that allows difficult issues to be discussed respectfully and thoughtfully.

Abraham Lincoln put it this way: "I don't like that man. I'm going to have to get to know him." In the workplace, we have lost sight of the value of spending time in conversations that are not directly related to the task at hand. Let's change that.

> *"One of the most beautiful qualities of true friendship is to understand and to be understood."*
>
> —Seneca, Roman philosopher

Don't wait for team building

To get the real power out of your meetings, it's imperative to get to know each other in a way that gives you permission to say or ask anything—in a way that makes challenging, back-and-forth conversation accessible. It may seem as if you know each other, but you probably don't—at least not in terms of what is possible. Your ability to be productive and to contribute to the organization is a function of not just how many people you know, but how many of them you can count on to be responsive to your questions, requests, and offers.

Professional friendships, like personal friendships, create a partnership you can each depend on as you work toward common goals in the organization. In addition, life can be tough unless you feel connected to others. Why not have this sense of connection be available at work?

A rich network of relationships changes your entire experience of work. Your sense of belonging increases proportionally with how many people you recognize and can say hello to when you see them. When you regard many colleagues as friends, it's easier to be yourself.

Your ability to work on cross-functional teams, in matrix organizations, or across organizational boundaries is enhanced by knowing lots of people. In addition, a team's performance is heightened when members get to know each other beyond what is expected.

You can deepen your relationships without waiting for special team-building events. Working on relationships requires deciding to make time for it. It's simple, but not easy. It means making a commitment, then shifting priorities to allow the time for making connections. You are busy—perhaps busier than you would like to be. Still, part of working in an organization demands that you find time to create and maintain the relationships you need to be successful. As Tom Scheuermann at Oregon State University puts it, "It's either pay now or pay later. If we 'pay' with spending a little time building relationships, we will avoid 'paying' later with having to re-explain things, deal with bruised egos, or handle confusion or colleagues who don't seem to care enough to deliver on time."

In the face of this reality, make spending time with your colleagues a priority. Making this small adjustment in your priorities can involve only a couple of hours a month, yet still make a real difference. The benefits of deeper relationships, while perhaps not immediately apparent, will allow for more effective communication and reciprocal support in both work and life.

Use your meetings to build your network

While making time for coffee is wonderful, the meetings you are already attending may be the best way to add to or enhance your relationships. I realize meetings are being booked back-to-back with little time for transit, let alone social conversation before or after. If you are in a position where you can do something about the stacking up of meetings, please do so. Even doing this once or twice a week can make a real difference over time. In the long run, the rewards will be substantial.

As the person leading, you can conduct your meetings in a way that builds trust, enables you to know one another in a more profound way, and brings appreciating each other to a new level. Focus on these four practices to develop relationships during the meeting:

- **Build some time in at the beginning for people to reconnect.**
  Have coffee available and let people know you'll be there fifteen minutes before the meeting starts. Then set aside ten minutes at the outset of the meeting, and invite several people to share what is going on in their lives.

- **Be thoughtful about getting more people into each discussion.** Invite people who have not spoken yet. Call on people who may have different views or who can help add clarity to the conversation.

- **Ensure the group is attentive when each person speaks.** Set up guidelines about technology and side conversations. If the group is distracted, ask the person who is speaking to wait a moment until people are ready.

- **Acknowledge the participation and value added when people contribute.** Use people's names. Note when they offer a view that wasn't in the conversation previously. Acknowledge when they cause you to think differently.

Learn to work the room in meetings

Traditionally we think of *working the room* as the act of circulating among people at a large gathering. In the context of meetings, it makes sense to look at working the room in a more focused way. Consider working the room to cover all of the conversations before and after a meeting that allow you to meet or reconnect with people.

This is not a skill set reserved for politicians or CEOs. It's a skill anyone will benefit from. The more people you know, the more access you have. The deeper each relationship goes, the easier it is to work together. Here's how to work the room in meetings:

Take the initiative. It begins with intention. Once you decide to focus on connecting with people, you'll find it comes naturally.

Arrive early and stay late. Introduce yourself to anyone you don't already know. If you know everyone, catch up with people you haven't seen for a while. Ask about their projects, their trips, their outside interests, their favorite sports teams, their families. Then listen with your full attention until they finish. After the meeting, hang around and ask a follow-up question on a topic that interested you in the meeting. Look for opportunities to walk to and from meetings with colleagues.

Greet people as they arrive. Don't worry about having a conversation with everyone, but do quickly connect—even if it is just saying their names and nodding at them across the table. In particular, look for new faces and include them. We can all remember being the new kid on the block and either how good it felt to be acknowledged or how diminishing it felt to be ignored.

Ask people to share about things that matter to them. This is the key piece in building a connection. Talking about the weather or sports won't do it. Listen for their interests, projects, and passions. You can show interest in a person without crossing personal boundaries. You don't have to probe into their personal lives. Ask about their projects or any other recent experience that fits. Be sure to listen fully. Ask follow-up questions that are of interest to you. Move beyond small talk to a conversation that allows you to know someone a little better.

Be interested. Keep your focus on the other person and what he or she shares. Don't worry about being interesting. Resist the temptation to turn the conversation to yourself. You must share to make this a partnership, but err on the side of listening rather than speaking. When you do this, you'll often find that people will reciprocate and want to get to know you as well.

Use people's names. Ask if you don't remember. Confident people acknowledge when they've forgotten: *"I'm sorry, I don't remember your* *name."* During the meeting, credit people by name for introducing new ideas or triggering your thinking. Refer to their earlier comments when appropriate.

Make notes on people you meet and what you discuss. This serves you in two ways: you will remember more, and the notes can serve to refresh your memory before future meetings. Focus on people you don't know well. Listen for what you can learn about them. What are they working on? What are they facing or dealing with? What are they excited about? You'll be surprised how much you learn when you are listening for it.

> **TRY THIS**
> ☐ Listen for what you can learn about people in each meeting.
> ☐ Notice the response of others when you are intentional about connecting with them.
> ☐ Leave each meeting with the name of someone with whom to follow up.

Overcome common connection hurdles

At this point, you're ready to spend more time connecting with people, but you may not be sure how to proceed. These are the questions that executive coaches typically encounter about creating relationships.

When do I find the time? Well, luckily, the gift you offer when you ask people how their kids did in the weekend soccer games takes only a few minutes. If you listen flat-out for three or four minutes, the conversation will have greater impact than this small investment of time suggests. People can say a lot in three or four minutes if you just listen.

How do I get comfortable meeting people? I get this. My conversational preference is still to be quiet and reflective. I rarely go to parties, and if Cindy signs us up to go to a wedding, I'm likely to find the first couple I know, sit down, and stay there for the entire evening. I'm certainly not going to go around the room meeting people—unless Cindy asks me to.

For example, as we drove from Minneapolis to Keokuk, Iowa, for Cindy's high school reunion, she asked me to go out of my way to meet and interact with as many people as I could. Why did she ask? First, she knows I'm good at working the room if I put my mind to it, and if I did so, she expected people would tell her what a great guy she is married to. Second, if I'm engaged with others, she doesn't have to worry about my enjoying myself and she can do her own thing. I agreed.

The first night was in a bar. Before I knew it, I was sitting at the end of the bar with another spouse who didn't attend this high school, watching the Cardinals play baseball on a big-screen television. It was perfect, and I was very comfortable. Then I saw Cindy across the room, and she motioned for me to join her. Time to work the room and make a difference.

Here's the point: If you're not already comfortable meeting people and engaging in conversation, you're not alone. But comfort is not a prerequisite. You can absolutely master working the room, and if you work in a large organization and want to be a solid contributor, it's required! With practice, your confidence will increase, and so will your comfort level.

How do I start a conversation with someone I don't know? In getting to know more people, building community, and deepening connections, the first step is always to engage people in conversation. The most common concern people share is, "But how do I start?"

3

RELATIONSHIPS

Start by simply being curious about people. Be interested in them. Give yourself permission to ask questions. Think beyond the typical questions, such as "How are you doing?" or "What's your job?" These questions don't often yield much.

If you ask people what they do in the organization, they will usually respond with a job title: "I'm the manufacturing engineer" or "I'm a software programmer." That gets you started, but it doesn't tell you much about what they do or how they feel about what they do for the organization. Follow up with, "Tell me about the projects you are working on that you are excited about or that you think might make a real impact on the organization's results."

Now you will be engaged in a conversation that is much richer, more specific, and easier for them to talk about. You have transcended the superficial.

You can broaden these questions to include their kids, their families, or outside interests they've got a lot of passion for. Family is an important part of people's lives and can lead to wonderful conversations. Most people appreciate an invitation to talk about themselves if they feel you are interested.

Still, be sensitive to the reactions your questions might generate. Sometimes people just don't feel comfortable talking about themselves. If you are listening intently, you can tell what kind of impact your question has and whether they are willing to get into that conversation. If you sense they're not willing, let it go.

How can I do this authentically? This is a question many people can relate to when talking about networking or working the room. At first, anything you try to change feels awkward, uncomfortable, mechanical—not right. You should expect this. When you change something, it should feel different. *Different* or *uncomfortable* are not the same as *wrong* or *artificial*. If your intention is to find a way to get into an interesting conversation with people, it is authentic—perhaps not comfortable, but it's authentic.

> "Authenticity is not something you have;
> it is something you choose."
>
> —Susan Scott, *Fierce Conversations*

TRY THIS

☐ Observe how other people open conversations. How do the people who excel at working the room begin their conversations with you? How do senior people interact with others in meetings?

☐ Develop a set of conversation openers that resonate with you. Here's a starter set:

- *I'd love to hear about your career. Tell me about your early days with the organization.*

- *What projects are you working on?*

- *Tell me about your family.*

- *What are your outside interests?*

- *Do you have any interesting trips planned for this year?*

Be willing to ask simple questions: *I have no idea what you do—can you explain that to me?*

What do I say when people ask me questions? Being able to talk on demand is a critical skill. When you are invited into a conversation, learn to respond in a way that is meaningful. When someone asks, "How was your weekend?" respond with, "It was great. We did x, y, and z." Don't take twenty minutes, but do take a minute or two and share what you did or what you most enjoyed. Then reciprocate, saying, "Thanks for asking. I'd like to hear about your weekend."

Whatever the topic, good conversation is like a dance. You lead with some personal remarks, and the other person follows because you've led the way. The idea here is to be genuine and friendly, not brilliant and captivating.

Do I have to be friends with everyone? We all have different definitions of what it means to be friends. I certainly don't mean to trivialize the notion of friendship. But here's my question: If you are going to spend time together, why not interact in a way that builds connection and relationship? Even if you will never see each other again, isn't there value in conversing in a way that builds connection?

A colleague expresses it this way: "If we don't become friends in the truest sense of the word, we will miss out on one of the opportunities that come with working in an organization."

Is it OK to keep work and personal life separate? It is fine to keep work and personal domains separate. Asking people about the past weekend or their plans for the upcoming weekend is common practice, but if people deflect your invitation to speak about it, don't push. Instead, ask about their projects and their work.

People are complex, and their lives are complicated. It's simple kindness to notice when people don't quite seem to be themselves. A gentle question about how they are doing will be appreciated even if they decline to answer.

"Everything OK?"

"You seem a bit preoccupied. Anything I can help with?"

Having compassion for what others might be dealing with is part of being great with people. You don't want to pry into their lives, but if you notice they are dealing with something away from work, you can simply offer your support. People will appreciate that you noticed and asked.

Without attention, relationships decline

We all have profound relationships that are based in wonderful shared experiences. Most work relationships do not have the same powerful background of experience, so they need more attention. Spending significant time together is important for some relationships. Working together in meetings will be enough for others. Making time for coffee once a month will keep other relationships in place. The question is: *What is required to keep each relationship at a level where conversation is easy?*

Ed Sullivan had a variety show on television in the sixties. A guest on one show set a series of plates spinning on poles. He started with one plate, got it spinning, then added another, then another. He eventually went back to the first plates and gave them another spin. As long as he could give some attention to each plate, he could keep them all spinning. If he couldn't get back to a plate in time, it would begin to slow, then wobble, and then fall.

Relationships are like this. If you don't check in with people now and then, the sense of connection fades. Even relationships with people you know well or with whom you have a profound connection need attention to keep them spinning.

RELATIONSHIPS

3

Checking in with people is a lost art

A university faculty member shared with me a young international student's question: "Why is it that everyone in America asks me how I am doing, and no one seems to care?"

This student is commenting on a practice that is so common we no longer notice—asking people questions without showing any interest in hearing the answer. This is a practice we should definitely reconsider.

Elle Allison, author of *Renewal Coaching*, asks people what makes them happy at work. The top answers:

- Being involved in a positive conversation.
- Producing something of value for someone else in the organization.
- Getting a couple of small things done from a long to-do list.
- Having a chance to talk about family.

Notice that two of these points relate to conversation. Begin to look for opportunities to check in with people you know. Ask them about their last business trip or their weekend or their latest project or their kids. Then stop and listen. Take advantage of every opportunity you encounter.

TRY THIS

☐ Encourage people to tell you more about themselves.

☐ Notice when people want you to talk.

☐ Invite someone to coffee.

Develop a system for keeping track of your relationships

As *Dilbert* creator Scott Adams said, it's systems, not goals, that make things happen. Setting up a system for tracking is one way to improve performance. For example, in golf, you might keep track of how many fairways you hit from the tee box and, if you miss, whether you miss right or left. Tracking something keeps it in your consciousness. In meetings, for example, you might keep track of these two things in order to train yourself to notice them:

- Who interrupts whom, and what happens to the conversation when this happens?

- When a conversation goes off track, how long before someone brings it back?

It's useful to apply this notion of having a system to relationships. Keeping track of people—noticing what's happening in their lives and checking in with them—helps you maintain and develop your relationships. With the wider network you need to have in your work life, it helps to have a system. For the long term, your memory is simply not good enough.

After presenting as a guest in a student leadership training program on the West Coast, I was approached by a college junior who asked if I would mentor her. Gabriella wanted to be more thoughtful and focused about where she spent her time and energy. She felt relationships were important and wanted that to be one of her areas of focus. I asked her to develop a simple spreadsheet of her current relationships, which might list their jobs, family members, interests, and current projects. I was expecting a list with maybe fifteen or twenty names. Two weeks later, she came back with a spreadsheet that had eighty-four names! She explained:

> My grandfather, Billy Flournoy, and his two brothers run
> Likely Land & Lovestock, a cattle ranch that has been in the
> family for 143 years. And for over fifty years, my grandfather
> has kept a diary of who he meets, what all he did that day, the
> weather, who he talked to, and anything notable to that day.
> Four years ago, I began doing the same thing. If you ask me
> who was at a meeting, I can tell you. If you ask me who went
> on a trip, I can tell you. If you ask me about their interests,
> I know some of them.

How many relationships do you need to create and maintain? I don't know what the number is for you or your position at work—thirty, fifty, a hundred? The number is likely larger than you can remember without a system. Some people advocate using a spread-sheet to keep track of the relationships in their lives; others use a daily journal. In any case, such a system for keeping track of your relationships allows you to build a basis for future conversations.

When I suggest this in class, usually someone argues that it seems inauthentic to have a system. However, we all keep contact lists on our phones or PCs. What I'm suggesting is adding basic notes that help you remember important things about the people you meet. This is not about getting ahead. This is not about manipulating peo-ple. This is simply a way to remember and add value to important business relationships. And ultimately this is about making it easier for them and for you to be effective when you work together.

Ask yourself several questions to identify the people with whom you need to create relationships:

- *With whom do I need a relationship in order to be successful in this job?*
- *Whose expertise would I like to have access to?*
- *Who would I like to mentor me?*
- *As I look five years ahead, who would it be helpful to know?*
- *Who have I already met and want to keep track of?*

Start with a simple diary of people you meet. Ask about their projects, weekends, trips, and families. Make notes on what you learn about the people in meetings and in hallway conversations. Start here, and after a month, reflect on where you are in your relationships. Then reread this section. In addition to continuing what you've been doing that works for you, add something new.

Perhaps you don't see yourself as a "relationship" person like Gabriella, or you are skeptical when Tom Peters says that relationships are all we have. I'd like to suggest that you can honor your past and your desire for comfort, yet still push yourself to be more relationship oriented.

Ultimately, checking in with people and developing new relationships is a choice. And yet I believe your ability to connect with people is important—at work, yes, but also in your neighborhood, in your community, and with your family.

Being wonderful with others is a skill that can not only be learned, but mastered. Just imagine what might become easier—what might become possible—if you were really good at creating and maintaining great relationships.

RELATIONSHIPS

3

TRY THIS

☐ Listen in a way that honors each person who speaks. Devote yourself to each of the conversations in which you participate. Hold back your questions and just listen. Use the phrase, *"Tell me more."* Stay silent when people finish a thought to see if they start speaking again.

☐ Recover the lost art of checking in with people. Ask people about their interests, their projects, their travels, their kids. It doesn't take much time. Ask a question, and then listen for three or four minutes.

☐ Learn to work the room. For many people, working the room and interacting with others in a wonderful, gracious way does not come naturally. That's fine, but it doesn't excuse you from getting good at this if you work in an organization.

☐ Keep track of your relationships. Maintaining a journal of people you meet and your conversations with them will help you remember.

☐ Reconnect with two people each week.

3
RELATIONSHIPS

" You can make more friends in two months
by being interested in other people
than in two years of trying
to get people interested in you. "

—Dale Carnegie
American writer and lecturer

" How we spend our days is, of course, how we spend our lives. "

—Annie Dillard
American writer

Decide
What Matters
and
Who Cares

Core ideas:

- Why meet? To talk about what matters with the people who care.
- Be vigilant about what gets on the agenda.
  - What possibilities are you working toward?
  - Talk about the right things.
  - Talk about fewer things.
- Invite only the people who must be there.
  - Eight is the target number.
  - Question the necessity to attend.
  - Ensure that people not attending stay informed.

"Never doubt that a small group of thoughtful, committed citizens can change the world; indeed, it's the only thing that ever has."

—Margaret Mead
American anthropologist

Why meet? To talk about what matters with the people who care

Management consultant and author Margaret Wheatley is interested in encouraging small groups to take on the issues they care about to make meaningful changes in their communities. She talks about small groups of people being able to make a big difference, and she uses the question, *"What matters and who cares?"* to help define a group's purpose in seeking change.

I like this in the context of meetings for three reasons: If you limit your meetings to discussions about what matters, your meetings will have more impact. If you invite only those most concerned, the conversations will be focused and productive. And you will also protect people's time—making sure the investment value is high for those attending and giving those not needed in the meeting more time for individual work.

When you are thoughtful about choosing what makes it onto the agenda and whom to invite, people will look forward to attending.

WHAT IF PEOPLE KNEW THAT:

- When you schedule a meeting, the meeting is necessary?
- You will not put something on the agenda unless it deserves the group's attention?
- They could decline if their attendance is not critical?
- If not invited, they could still provide input?
- You have a deep respect for their time?

Here's the situation. Technology has made it so easy to schedule a meeting. You simply hit the meeting button, select the participants, and it appears on their calendars. Cool! And maddening!

Meanwhile, employees continue to add work hours to their days, often taking work home at the expense of family and friends and even health. Many organizations are realizing there is a big downside associated with the number of hours people are working.

Still, meetings remain the primary way to make progress on goals, to resolve issues, and to get projects off the ground. *Meetings are essential, and they are not going away.* So what we need is a breakthrough in how many hours we spend in meetings.

Some organizations are trying bold moves, such as declaring there will be no meetings on Friday. I love bold moves. They disrupt the way people think by calling attention to problems in a dramatic way. Doing this for a few months is long enough for people to get back in touch with what it is like to have more discretionary time during the day. At some point, however, you want people to be able to schedule meetings whenever they're needed—even on a Friday—because meetings make things happen.

It is possible to reduce the number of meetings by making it a priority to do so. Tracking how many meetings you have and then working to reduce that number will result in fewer meetings.

This book takes a different approach, however. The intention here is to make every conversation in every meeting count, leading to fewer hours spent in meetings overall.

How do you do this? As a supervisor, manager, or project leader, it begins with being more thoughtful about your agenda and about who should be part of the conversation.

Be vigilant about what gets on the agenda

I remember being in the office of the CEO of a Fortune 100 company. I was there to ask him to speak at a leadership seminar. He pulled open his desk drawer and took out a list. "I appreciate the invitation. I'm sure the seminar is worthwhile. But this is how I decide where I am going to put my time and energy. This is my list of imperatives for the year. If you can show me how speaking at your event will forward one or more of these imperatives, I'll do it. If you can't, I won't."

Most managers and leadership teams could benefit from this kind of rigor in deciding what gets their time and attention in meetings. Some organizations use different language for where they focus their resources, time, and energy: *strategic intent, imperatives, vital few, ambitions, key initiatives*. By whatever name, these provide a point of choice for where to spend energy and time.

Appendix A includes a meeting design for setting goals and determining your focus, including targeted questions to help define your own list of imperatives. Take the time to identify what matters, then aim every meeting at making progress on these issues. Otherwise, why meet?

What possibilities are you working toward?

There is a difference in life between acting out of obligation or out of inspiration. Inspiration is shaped by having some possibility in mind—seeing the connection between how you are spending your time and a desirable future that doesn't exist right now.

Bob Rotella, in his book *Golf Is Not a Game of Perfect*, recalls a conversation with golfing legend, Byron Nelson. "When I was a young man, my dream was to own a ranch. Golf was the only way I was going to get that ranch. And every tournament I played in, I was going after a piece of it."

Compelling futures are like that—they inspire action. Effective people, groups, and organizations work hard to make sure they are spending their time on things that matter.

Consider the time in meetings to be precious. Ensure that anyone who requests time on the agenda is respectful of the group's time. There are so many demands on our time and energy. Imagine how differently we might spend our time if we asked ourselves these questions each day:

- *What am I creating with how I am spending my time?*
- *What set of possibilities is associated with this activity?*

As a supervisor or manager, ask similar questions about what you are putting on the agenda for your meetings. There should be a connection between what you talk about in meetings and what the organization is trying to accomplish. The richer the possibility you can link to your group's work, the more fulfilling that work will be.

Talk about the right things

One view of leadership says it is about creating clarity, future, and focus. Usually people think about this statement in terms of setting strategic direction and goals for the organization. Tactically, it means keeping meetings focused on the right things.

A worldwide manufacturing engineering group with thirty members asked me to observe their conversations and suggest how they might improve their meetings. This group met eight hours a month with the goal to improve worldwide manufacturing excellence. Before I went to observe, I asked to see their agendas from the previous six meetings. In those meetings, they had spent only 10 percent of their time discussing manufacturing excellence. They had spent four hours deciding whether one unit could reward people for perfect attendance. They had spent another two hours deciding what to do about an employee who kept parking in a no-parking zone.

As so often happens, this group of talented managers got pulled into short-term problem solving or low-level distractions rather than spending the time to go deeper into topics that have long-term leverage. They'd also slipped into a pattern of going lightly over ten to twelve agenda items rather than doing meaningful work on a few.

It doesn't help to work on improving your meetings if you are talking about the wrong things.

What merits time on the agenda?

These are the overarching questions:

- *What are the conversations we as a group need to have?*
- *Given what this group is expected to accomplish and given what we think we might produce by working together in a remarkable way, what should we be discussing?*

The following conversations are likely candidates:

Discussing progress on the team's most critical goals and initiatives should be first choice, especially if progress is in jeopardy.

Making decisions that require the best thinking and full ownership of the group should also be high on the priority list.

Providing input to a manager or colleague who has a significant issue and has asked for suggestions is another area where the experience of the group adds value.

4

WHAT MATTERS

Gaining clarity on an organizational problem so it can be handed off to a smaller working group is part of the work of larger groups.

Discussing strategic topics such as talent reviews, organizational restructuring, or hiring decisions keeps the organization positioned for the future.

Discussing complex issues generates shared understanding within the group. Organizational values and the culture itself are honed by discussing fundamental topics such as transparency, inclusion, integrity, and ethics.

Training in short, powerful segments on topics the team must embrace is also worthy of a group's time.

Bottom line: Don't meet just because you are a group and you've "always had a weekly staff meeting." Ask this question: *In your regular meetings, are you honoring the time of group members by discussing things that matter?* It's an important question, and in my experience, few groups could answer in the affirmative. If you want to meet on a regular basis, fine. Just make sure you are thoughtful about the agenda for each and every meeting.

Talk about fewer things

Keep the number of items on the agenda as small as possible. There will be less pressure to rush through the agenda if you have fewer items, and participants will be able to focus on each conversation if there are not ten topics to divide their attention.

A good guideline is two meaningful topics per hour. That means in a three-hour meeting, you might have six agenda items. If a topic warrants the time and attention of the talent in the meeting, then it deserves enough time to do thorough work. You must have enough time to discuss the topic, reach alignment, and agree on next steps.

The criteria remain the same regardless of the meeting topic: *Are you doing complete work on each topic? Does each conversation lead to clarity and alignment about what happens next?*

Make staff meetings count

A colleague shared that each day begins with a staff meeting that has no agenda and is little more than listening to her boss for forty-five minutes while wishing she could get to the work sitting back on her desk.

Staff meetings seem like a good thing to have. They are a chance to connect with each other, check in on how things are going, and maintain the sense of being a group that is working together. Fair enough. No doubt your intentions are good, but stop and be honest about what you are producing by meeting.

Here's a suggestion: Keep the meeting on the calendar as scheduled. Then each week, determine whether you have a good reason for meeting. If not, cancel. If yes, limit the meeting to the amount of time needed to discuss the topic that requires the group's attention. When you cancel or shorten the meeting, everyone will appreciate the time you've given them back to focus on their individual work.

4
WHAT MATTERS

Be careful about information and group sharing

Be vigilant about what is not a good use of the whole group's time. Keep information sharing to a minimum. In a three-hour meeting, it's fine to take fifteen minutes to cover administrative items or share information, but most information can be sent via e-mail or memo.

Group sharing is another common practice to watch out for—going around the table and giving everyone a few minutes to share. This is a well-intended notion that can easily drift into a lot of time spent not being productive. If you love this practice, just sharpen it up with the directive for people to be concise and limit their comments to what honors the group's time.

Invite only the people who must be there

This is the "Who cares" part of the question: *Who should be part of the conversation in order to accomplish the outcomes defined in the agenda?* Whose presence is **necessary** for the topics to be discussed and handled? Who must be there to get the work done? Who, if they can't attend, means you might as well reschedule?

Once you have the core group committed to attending, you can ask, *Is there anyone else with an interest or potential contribution who merits an invitation to this meeting?* One caveat: less is more.

When looking at who else to invite, consider people:

- with organizational knowledge and history who can point out flaws in your approach,
- whose support is so vital they must be involved,
- who have a perspective that no one else in the room can represent,

- who are building their knowledge base and the topics in this meeting would help, or

- who have questions or concerns about the project and being part of the conversation would be the most effective way to alleviate them.

Eight is the target number

Stanford management science and organizational behavior professor Robert Sutton writes about the troubles that arise when groups get too large. He compares it to booking a table for ten or fifteen people at a restaurant: "It is difficult, perhaps downright impossible, to have a coherent and emotionally satisfying conversation that engages each member of the party all at once. Typically, the group breaks into a series of smaller conversations or a few people do all the talking and the others say little or nothing." His summary of research on effective group size affirms that anything over ten gets into trouble. He believes seven—plus or minus one—is the magical number. Close enough!

> *"I find it easier to be myself in small groups."*
> —Fortune 100 CEO

Five to eight is the best size for most working groups—small enough to sit in intimate physical proximity, easy to get everyone's views considered, enough differing views and experience to ensure a robust discussion, and small enough to assure a candid and authentic conversation. When you have remote attendees, keeping the group small is even more important, so they can feel connected and be brought into the conversation.

Discussing something in groups of four or five is easy. If you go beyond eight, people become more careful in what they say, and there is simply less time for everyone to speak. Expand this to twenty, and you can see the problem.

Bottom line: Remember that small groups are far more effective than large groups. To be successful, invite the minimum number of people—ideally no more than eight. Invite only the people who must be there. If you are thoughtful about who should attend a meeting, there will be fewer meetings for many people.

"Sure, why not?"

It's easy to drift over time into a situation where you have people attending leadership team meetings who don't need to be there—people who like the prestige that comes with being included, who represent groups that no one else does, whom you need for thirty minutes of a three-hour meeting, who are sitting in for someone else, or who used to be vital to the group but no longer are.

It's almost as if when someone suggests inviting someone, the default response is, "Sure, why not?" This drift has three downside risks:

- The group gets too large to interact effectively.

- Agenda items become less about real work and more about information sharing and updates.

- Eventually, a "kitchen cabinet" group ends up addressing the topics that are difficult to deal with in the larger group, thereby defeating the purpose.

Think of it this way: each person who is added to the group adds a degree of difficulty in having efficient, authentic conversations.

Question the necessity to attend

I recall working with Keith, a senior executive who asked for help in making time for four new goals: learn Spanish, mentor new hires, catch up on reading, and connect with employees at locations he rarely visited. After getting clear about the value he associated with each goal, I asked Keith to find a way to carve eight hours out of his current weekly schedule, beginning the next week, arguing that if one doesn't devote substantial time to new projects, it won't be long before they wither and die out.

The next week, he reported that after our call, he grumbled to his assistant that he had been asked to carve eight hours out of his next week's schedule—an impossible task. His assistant replied, "I can do that for you. You are in fifteen hour-long meetings every week. Just give me permission to tell those folks they get you for thirty minutes, and they can decide what part of the meeting they want you for. I can also say you would like them to decide each week if they need you to attend."

It never occurred to this senior manager to question his time in meetings; he wanted to be supportive of each person who asked for his participation. As you can imagine, Keith's experience created a new perspective on attending meetings, not only for him, but for his entire organization.

In the same way, give your people permission to question whether their attendance is necessary. Give them permission to protect their time, and be clear about how their attendance will be constructive. You also want to protect your people by not scheduling meetings during their most productive or creative times of day. Be thoughtful about interrupting their work with a meeting.

In addition, part of being an effective meeting participant is realizing that you have the right to ask for what you need, and that includes questioning whether you must attend. Sure, there are some meetings you won't have permission to decline. But most managers will be supportive if you ask to know what part of the meeting requires your participation or whether the agenda could be adjusted to fit your schedule.

If you choose not to attend a meeting, you have certain responsibilities to the group and to the person leading the meeting. These include:

- Reviewing the agenda and giving your input to someone who will be attending.

- Asking someone to take notes and provide an update on the meeting afterward.

- Giving the leader permission to assign you work.

- Agreeing to align with any decisions that are made.

You get the idea: if you don't attend, you are still responsible for making the meeting successful.

TRY THIS

☐ For every meeting, list the possibilities and value associated with each topic on the agenda.

☐ Make a list of what matters to your group or organization and compare it to your agenda topics for the last three weeks.

☐ Give people permission to question whether their attendance is required.

Ensure that people not attending stay informed

Ask this question when you are preparing for and at the end of every meeting: *Who would like to know about what was discussed and decided?*

If you are more thoughtful about whom you invite—erring on the side of fewer people—you want to take care of those who are not invited. What is the best way to consult with them and get their input before the meeting? How will you bring them up to speed on the conversation after the meeting? How will you get their reactions or feedback?

Letting the appropriate people know beforehand about your meeting gives them a chance to provide input or make a case for attending.

It's also important to prepare a summary of the meeting that will be clear to those who don't attend. For more on keeping the conversation alive through meeting notes, see strategy 6, page 141.

4

WHAT MATTERS

Who is feeling disenfranchised?

At the end of each monthly meeting of a large school district, the leadership team considered this question: *Who in our district might be feeling disenfranchised right now, and what should we do about it?*

One risk of limiting who attends a meeting is furthering the disconnect between the people involved in the decision making of the organization and the individuals and groups who feel they are on the outside looking in. If you want the entire organization on your side, you must constantly look for who might be feeling left out and find a way to include and communicate with them.

"Design is not just what it looks
like and feels like.
Design is how it works."

—Steve Jobs
Apple founder

Design
Each Conversation

Core ideas:

- A meeting is, in essence, a series of conversations.
  - To be effective, conversations should be designed.
  - Begin with the *what* and *how* of design.
- Conversation design includes setup, process steps, and closure.
- Set the stage to have the conversation.
- Process steps map the path to follow.
- Closure wraps up the conversation.
- Design matters regardless of group size or structure: one-on-one meetings, large group meetings, or virtual meetings.

"Great meetings don't just happen—they're designed. Producing a great meeting is a lot like producing a great product. You don't just build it. You think about it, plan it, and design it."

—Michael Begeman
3M Meeting Network,
quoted in *Fast Company*

A meeting is, in essence, a series of conversations

One of my mentors gave me this perspective when I was preparing to lead a day-long retreat for the United Way. "Paul, this is not mysterious. A retreat or any meeting is just a series of conversations. If you are clear about what the group must discuss and the best way to talk about each of the topics, you'll have your design."

Effective meetings happen when you have a design prepared for each conversation and someone leading the meeting who is able to take advantage of having the design as a road map to follow.

You can design and lead meetings that people look forward to attending—meetings they won't want to miss. This is not only possible, it's not all that difficult. And the payoff will be greater productivity and much shorter meetings.

To be effective, conversations should be designed

A leadership group in Brazil asked for guidance about conducting virtual meetings because they rarely were able to meet in the same location. I asked them to allow me to observe as they worked through two topics during a face-to-face meeting. Observing a group lets me see what they do that works and identify missing pieces that would be useful to add. It also provides specific points in the conversation to refer to when sharing my impressions.

After about sixty minutes of observation, I respectfully told them that virtual meetings would be difficult because they were not even close to being effective when they were in the same room. They laughed and agreed. I appreciated their willingness to hear candid feedback—it's always rewarding when a group is more interested in getting better than pretending they already know everything.

A number of issues were revealed in that hour. The vice president was hampered by trying to lead the meeting, listen to the conversation, and insert his own comments. People interrupted, spoke over one another, and did not acknowledge the remarks of others. Individuals became defensive when their comments were ignored or challenged.

But the number one problem, which is true of many meetings, was the lack of a clear and visible set of process steps for working through each of the topics on the agenda. Determining the best way to discuss and work on each topic was the missing piece. Listing these steps on a whiteboard or in a handout before the discussion began would have helped ensure that everyone's comments were relevant, kept the conversation on track, and prevented people from leaving with a sense that this was one more meeting that wasn't well-run or productive.

Here's another example to help explain what I mean. A group of university faculty were meeting to discuss deficiencies that Ph.D. students needed to address before completing their studies. Doctoral candidates can be admitted into graduate programs without all the required prerequisites, but with an understanding that those shortcomings will be resolved before completing the dissertation. For a variety of reasons, some deficiencies were not resolved.

This group of faculty had already met several times on this issue without making progress. Instead, their interactions produced tension that was fracturing relationships.

5

DESIGN

I asked them to try again while I observed. The conversation went something like this:

> PROFESSOR A: "I really don't think it's anybody's business how I handle the academic requirements of my students."

> ADMINISTRATOR A: "Well, if it were just a few cases, I wouldn't be concerned."

> PROFESSOR B: "There are some deficiencies that need to be made up, but frankly, some of them aren't important."

> PROFESSOR C: "How big is the problem?"

> PROFESSOR A: "The problem isn't the issue. Who has decision rights is what matters."

> PROFESSOR C: "I know, but are we talking about three students or fifteen students, and are we talking about one or two deficiencies or five or more?"

> PROFESSOR D: "Have we looked at what other universities are doing?"

At this point, the conversation just began recycling, with people saying the same things over and over with increasing frustration and drama. I interrupted and acknowledged them for their commitment to their individual students, for their candor and the clarity of their speaking, and for their willingness to let me observe.

Then I suggested the following process steps as a path forward:

1. Begin by listing the key elements of the situation and check to see if any elements had been missed or not yet mentioned.

2. Once we agree on the elements, describe each clearly.

3. Then ask for a small group to work on the issue offline, with the commitment that the full group has the right to amend the small group's work before any decisions are made.

We then captured in writing the elements of the situation already expressed and added new elements:

- What exactly is the problem? Can we identify the number of students and deficiencies for each?

- Who has decision rights for each student? Faculty? The administration?

- What are other colleges and universities doing?

- What is the provost's position on this?

Everyone agreed these were the questions to be answered, and four people volunteered to work offline and return to the group with not only the answers to these questions, but with suggestions for resolving the issue. Then I asked the three faculty members who were most vocal if they were willing to be consulted by the working group so their concerns and ideas would be fully heard and included. They agreed.

This group needed three things to get to the desired result:

1. a logical way to work through the conversation,

2. someone to capture each comment, and

3. a commitment that the process would remain open until everyone was satisfied with the solution.

Perhaps you recall similar meetings. They happen all the time. Good, committed, bright people lack the knowledge of how to work through difficult issues—at least not without considerable struggle. What makes it so difficult? These are the usual culprits:

- No one captures what is being said in an orderly way so people feel their comments won't be lost or disregarded.

- No one listens to each person attentively so they feel as if they have been heard.

- Groups often develop norms of interrupting and talking over one another.

- And, most importantly, groups attempt to work through an issue without a clear, step-by-step process being agreed to first.

Sure, it would be great if people listened and were gracious with each other—even difficult conversations don't have to be disagreeable. But the missing piece is usually a design for the process.

If you love sports, you might think of the design for a meeting as similar to having a good "game plan." A team with a good game plan will not only be more likely to succeed, but the game will also be more enjoyable for those participating.

Begin with the *what* and *how* of design

Each conversation in a meeting is made up of content—the "what" that is to be discussed—and process—the "how" it will be discussed. An agenda provides a list of the content to be discussed in a meeting, and the design defines the process—the step-by-step approach that will get you to the desired outcome for each item on the agenda.

The first part of design, then, is answering two content questions:

- *What conversations do we need to have together?*
- *What do we want to achieve in each conversation?*

The first question is discussed in the previous strategy, "Decide What Matters and Who Cares." The second question helps you define what you are trying to achieve as a result of the conversation. Where do you want to be at the end of twenty or forty minutes? Clarity about this outcome shapes your design. I'm referring here to the outcome for the discussion, not necessarily an "out-in-the-world" outcome. For example, if you are discussing the start of a capital campaign for a university, the total dollars to be raised would be the out-in-the-world outcome. The outcome for this meeting might be agreeing on a time line, milestones, and a working committee.

5

DESIGN

Examine each conversation topic

To begin your design process, each item on the agenda should be examined to determine the following:

Who is the **owner**?

Who requested time on the agenda for it? This is the person you will ask to set the stage for discussing the topic and to wrap up the discussion at the end. (See more about meeting roles in appendix D, page 327.)

What are the desired **outcomes**?

Where do you want to be at the end of the discussion? Specific objectives for each discussion help participants contribute comments and questions that are relevant. Defining the outcomes up front also gives people clarity about where the conversation is intended to finish.

How much **time** is required?

How long will it take to work through this issue? Start with thinking in terms of twenty-minute blocks. One reason to schedule fewer agenda items in a meeting is to allow you to take more time for a discussion if necessary. Start by scheduling the amount of time you think the group will require if people stay on track and work effectively. This provides a realistic time frame yet creates just the right amount of tension to stay on track and keep comments relevant. You can always add five or ten minutes if necessary to complete your topic. People also feel their time is being well spent if they have a sense of getting things done in a deliberate, efficient way.

> **PARKINSON'S LAW:** *Work expands so as to fill the time available for its completion.*
>
> —C. Northcote Parkinson, British naval historian and author
>
> **THROOP'S COROLLARY TO PARKINSON'S LAW:** *To keep work from expanding to fill all your time, you must strictly limit the time available for its completion.*
>
> —Kelvin R. Throop III, a character in R.A.J. Phillips'
> *Analog Science Fiction and Science Fact*

5

DESIGN

What **input** do you seek?

What are you looking for from participants? Being clear up front about what you want from the group will help keep the conversation on track. It also lets the group know how best to contribute. Sometimes you are looking for ideas. Sometimes you want to identify potential risks. Other times you are looking for alignment and you want everyone to identify anything that might keep them from aligning.

What is the best **process**?

What is the best way to work through each conversation toward accomplishing its desired outcome? Most topics benefit from having a clear path to follow as the group works through the discussion toward the desired result. (This is discussed more thoroughly on pages 97–109.)

What **preparation** would be helpful?

In addition to the agenda, what would be helpful for participants to receive ahead of time in order to prepare for discussing this topic? You can't expect people to read through anything during a meeting and provide useful insights. The quality of many discussions is dependent on the group's having time to reflect on the topic and outcomes prior to the meeting.

Who should **lead** the conversation?

Consider having someone manage the discussion of this topic other than the person who called the meeting or requested time on the agenda. For most conversations, it's best for the owner of the topic to be able to focus on listening to the group rather than managing the discussion. (You'll find more on this in "Guidelines for Managers," pages 242–246.)

What is the **group size** and **structure**?

How many people will attend? How will you be meeting? Groups larger than eight and groups meeting virtually especially benefit from visible process steps, such as a chart or handout, to help focus people's comments. Group size and structure also affect leading the meeting. A few more design considerations can be found on pages 112–117.

Agenda order

The order of agenda topics should be determined by these factors:

- Is there a natural sequence between some topics? Do some build on what gets produced in others?

- Can topics be ordered in a way to give people a change of pace, perhaps tackling a tough topic first, followed by one that is less challenging?

- Will anyone critical to a topic be absent during portions of the meeting? If so, set that topic at the beginning or end of the agenda, as appropriate.

Conversation design includes setup, process steps, and closure

There are three fundamental design elements for conducting any conversation: setup, process steps, and closure. These involve introducing the topic and how it will be discussed and defining the desired outcomes (setup), working through the discussion toward the desired outcome (process), and then wrapping up the conversation (closure). Think of setup and closure as the bookends for the step-by-step process that is the working part of the discussion. The form below outlines this structure:

The Basic Structure of a Conversation

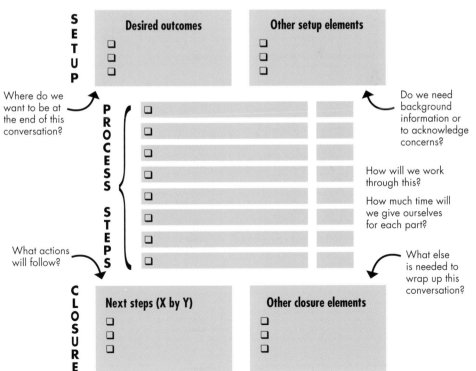

SETUP

Desired outcomes

Other setup elements

Where do we want to be at the end of this conversation?

PROCESS STEPS

Do we need background information or to acknowledge concerns?

How will we work through this?

How much time will we give ourselves for each part?

What actions will follow?

What else is needed to wrap up this conversation?

CLOSURE

Next steps (X by Y)

Other closure elements

Faculty example

Let's see how the elements from the faculty discussion on academic deficiencies would fit into this format:

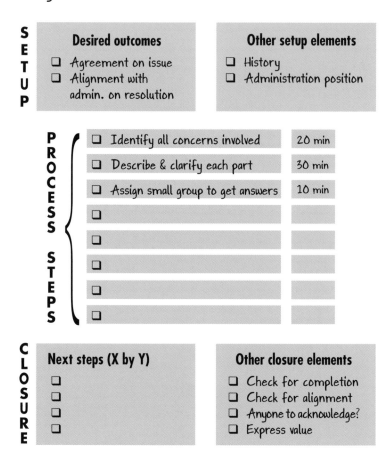

Agenda Item 1: Doctoral candidate deficiencies

S E T U P

Desired outcomes
- ❑ Agreement on issue
- ❑ Alignment with admin. on resolution

Other setup elements
- ❑ History
- ❑ Administration position

P R O C E S S   S T E P S

❑ Identify all concerns involved	20 min
❑ Describe & clarify each part	30 min
❑ Assign small group to get answers	10 min
❑	
❑	
❑	
❑	
❑	

C L O S U R E

Next steps (X by Y)
- ❑
- ❑
- ❑
- ❑

Other closure elements
- ❑ Check for completion
- ❑ Check for alignment
- ❑ Anyone to acknowledge?
- ❑ Express value

5

DESIGN

Set the stage to have the conversation

The setup essentially lets people know where you are going and how you are going to get there. The key element of the setup is defining the outcomes: *Where do you want to be at the end of the time allotted for this agenda item?*

Here's a brief setup for the faculty discussion:

> *"Let's review where we stand on the graduate student deficiencies. First, let's take twenty minutes and make sure we have each of the issues identified. Then, let's work through the issues and determine where each of us stands on them. Then we can determine the best way to address each issue. If we can resolve an issue here, fine; if not, we'll ask a small group to work on these and return with recommendations by next Tuesday. Does this make sense?"*

Many conversations are straightforward and, if you have a small group, it's only necessary to state the desired outcomes and the amount of time you anticipate spending on the conversation. This example includes a statement of the process steps to be followed.

Other topics might require you to include more background in the setup. For example, most budgeting discussions include refreshing everyone about the time line and how the budget process works. In addition, more time might be needed in the process steps for answering questions to ensure understanding by group members, especially those new to the organization.

Additional setup elements might include:

- Recapping how today's conversation fits into a larger picture or longer time frame.
- Providing an update on what has been done so far.

- Acknowledging concerns that you know exist within the group.

- Asking the organizational leader to state where he or she stands on the issue so people are not wondering.

- Clarifying what you need from the group if it is not obvious.

Setup elements for each topic

Define outcomes:

- What do you want to produce?

- Where do you want to be at the end of the discussion?

- What input are you seeking from participants?

Provide background:

- What is needed to bring people up to speed?

- Why are we having this conversation?

Acknowledge concerns:

- Any concerns you have coming in.

- Any concerns you expect participants might have.

Explain process:

- What process steps will we use?

- How much time will we allow for this conversation?

- Do we need to track this conversation visually (charts)?

- How will we capture and share this conversation (summary)?

Process steps map the path to follow

Thinking of the meeting as a series of conversations reminds you that working through a topic means having a thoughtful conversation about it, and that conversation will be easier if you follow a specific set of steps rather than jump all over the place. The beauty of having a systematic path is that it becomes much easier to keep the conversation on track, and staying on track correlates with better outcomes and shorter meetings.

Six designs cover most meeting conversations

A review of some forty designs I'd created for day-long retreats revealed six conversation designs that were used most often:

1. **Checking progress** on projects, goals, or initiatives
2. **Requesting input** from the group
3. **Responding to a problem**
4. **Starting a project**
5. **Making a decision**
6. **Creating alignment** for a goal, decision, or plan

There isn't a right set of process steps or the perfect sequence, so don't get locked in on "the only way" to discuss an issue. The six basic designs give you a starting place. Remember to think of them as the steps you will use to work through a topic. You can add steps, delete steps, or express them differently.

Let's look at these six designs more closely. Each contains a number of steps that provide a systematic way of working through the conversation. The key steps are defined in the numbered lists. Once the steps are defined, then it's time to focus on designing the questions that will get you to these objectives. You'll find the questions for each design in the shaded boxes labeled "Process steps."

You may notice that some questions could be included in the setup for the conversation, and others could be part of the closure. The three parts of the conversation design—setup, process steps, and closure—may overlap, which is natural as conversations unfold. The key is to be sure each part is present.

Checking progress

This is an important conversation—following up to ensure that all important projects, initiatives, task forces, or committees are making the desired progress. What's typical is to do quick, ten-minute updates rather than thorough twenty- to thirty-minute discussions with the project leader. Short updates can be done via e-mail; this design is for a conversation that allows time to discuss the project and fully clarify where it stands.

If you want to get up-to-date on how things are going on a project, these are the steps to work through to get the whole picture:

1. Describe the current status of the project using key variables such as schedule, cost, resource allocation, quality, and so on. The intent is to answer questions about where the project stands now.

2. Give everyone a chance to ask anything about the status of the project or initiative. Make sure everyone is clear about the status and has an opportunity to ask one another questions to help clarify where things stand.

3. Assess the status in relation to intended goals in terms of the key variables. In particular, you are looking for where the project is behind schedule or is facing difficulty.

4. Give people a chance to voice concerns or share problems that might otherwise remain hidden; make sure all issues are brought into the open.

5. Agree on a set of actions that will satisfy everyone in the group about what will be done next. Get specific commitments from people to take responsibility for these next steps, including a time line for completion.

6. Set a date to check progress again. Following up is essential to ensuring continued progress. Put it on the calendar to keep the project visible.

5

DESIGN

PROCESS STEPS FOR CHECKING PROGRESS

- Where do we stand on this project?
- What questions does the group have about where the project stands?
- Is our progress to date where we intend it to be?
- What concerns, ideas, or reactions do we have?
- What are the next steps or actions we should take?
- When does it make sense to schedule the next progress update?

Requesting input

One way to leverage the thinking of a group is to fully describe a problem or situation and then assign further work to a small group. This might involve a problem that affects the entire leadership team, or it can be an issue for one member who would like to get the thinking of colleagues.

When you need input from a group to describe or analyze a situation, these are the steps to work through in the conversation:

1. Describe the current situation or what has happened until now. This step brings everyone up to date.

2. Explain your viewpoint about the situation and your questions for the group. Define the input you need from them—ideas, questions, or concerns. This gives the group a starting place and an understanding of your current thinking. If you're concerned about overly directing where the conversation goes, you can reverse the order of steps 2 and 3.

3. Open the conversation to the group to get their reactions, questions, and ideas. This is the group's chance to influence your thinking.

4. Acknowledge what people say and keep asking for more until the group winds down. This allows people to feel heard and encourages additional ideas. Sometimes the ideas that emerge when you continue to ask are better than the initial ones people express.

5. Check one last time for any other input. In particular, check with people who haven't spoken yet.

6. Summarize what you heard and are taking away from the conversation.

7. Explain what you plan to do with their input. This honors the group's contributions and lets them know which of their ideas will be utilized and which will not.

8. Check with the group to see if anyone has reservations about the next steps you propose. This is part of checking for alignment.

PROCESS STEPS FOR REQUESTING INPUT

- Here's the situation.
- These are my thoughts about the situation.
- What do you think? Questions? Ideas? Concerns?
- What else? (Please keep adding to the conversation.)
- Anything else? (I sense everything has been expressed.)
- OK, here's what I've heard.
- Here's what I suggest we do.
- Is everyone OK with this?

5

DESIGN

Responding to a problem

Problems deserve and benefit from the thinking of the group, because often individual thinking is blurred by personal reactions to what has happened. In fact, when we take things personally, we lose our ability to think clearly. One of the most powerful ways to be empowered in the face of a problem is to ask the group to help think it through.

When a problem has occurred and you need the wisdom of the group to help resolve it, these are the steps to work through in the conversation:

1. Describe the situation thoroughly—everything you know for sure. Complete an accurate picture of exactly what has happened. Doing this first will decrease the number of clarifying questions that might come later. It also ensures that the rest of the steps are focused on the resolution.

2. List the questions to be answered to more fully understand the situation and gain new insight. In step one, you get clear about what you know. This step provides clarity about what you don't know.

3. Define what should be considered and accounted for before you make decisions. Determine a set of criteria to evaluate the options you will consider.

4. Explore the options available for responding to the problem. You may also identify people who may be able to provide additional options.

5. Open the conversation for additional thoughts. You don't want to miss other ideas, questions, or concerns the group has not yet expressed. There may not be many, but they could be important.

6. Given where you are at the end of this conversation, decide what you will do next. List the specific actions to be taken and note the names of any people who should be informed or consulted. Also, determine who will follow the progress of the actions agreed upon to ensure they get done.

PROCESS STEPS FOR RESPONDING TO A PROBLEM

- What do we know?
- What questions are to be answered?
- What criteria should shape our response?
- What are our options?
- Are there other thoughts?
- What will we do? What are the next steps?

Starting a project

Starting a new project is a time to go slow and get it right. Time spent up front on the design and formulation of a project will pay off. Getting a project off the ground requires defining the overall project, including outcomes, time line, milestones, and next steps. Here is the process to work through in the conversation:

1. Define the overall outcomes you have committed to achieve. These are the specific, measurable results that the project is designed to produce—the outcomes that the organization will be expecting.

2. Describe what success looks like—what you want to be true at the end of this project. You want a complete definition of each outcome so it is clear and fully described.

3. From start to finish, set the important dates for accomplishing the steps that will help frame the project. This is the time line that maps the project against the reality of a calendar so people can see how this fits into their other work demands.

4. Determine the milestones that would give you a sense of progress and urgency from beginning to end. Often the end date of a project is so far out, there isn't any real urgency to get started. Milestones not only provide a viable path to the end, they force people to stay focused from the beginning of the project.

5. Determine what resources are required. List everything that comes to mind as you think about how you will make this happen. The intent is to get as close as you can to knowing what resources will be required so they can be planned for early on.

6. Define the relationships you will develop—the people you want on your side or those you need access to. These are

relationships with people outside of the project team who have something to contribute or a stake in the outcome.

7. Thinking of the next few weeks, define the set of actions that will give you a sense of momentum. This gets you off to a great start. Outcomes, milestones, and time lines shape the project. The next two or three weeks of action are critical to a good start-up.

8. If you want this to succeed, you need to follow up, follow up, and follow up, so decide when and how often it make sense for you to check progress. Good project management includes follow-up and asking questions for clarification. That's not a lack of trust or micromanaging. It's acknowledging that people are busy, things happen, and if you don't follow up, you'll get behind and be disappointed. Better to follow closely and thoughtfully.

5

DESIGN

PROCESS STEPS FOR STARTING A PROJECT

- What have we committed to do?
- What specifically are the outcomes?
- What's the time line?
- What milestones make sense?
- What will it take to produce this?
- What relationships should we ensure are in place?
- What actions will get us off to a great start?
- When should we check in with how the start-up is going?

Making a decision

When people speak about the need for transparency, one of the areas they are pointing at is decision making. Adding decision making to your meetings also allows more people to develop ownership for decisions made there. These are the steps to work through in reaching a group decision:

1. Clearly state the decision required so people know what they are determining in this conversation.

2. Discuss who has decision rights and the process to be used in making the decision. Knowing up front who has decision rights helps people better understand how to contribute to the conversation.

3. Outline the criteria for a successful outcome and how you will determine which option is best. Explore what the decision must produce or provide for. Consider how this decision will impact what's important to you.

4. Define all the options you have. Consider who might know of other options and get their input.

5. Outline the upsides and downsides associated with each option. This assessment of potential benefits and risks is designed to get the group to thoughtfully express support or concerns for each option.

6. Make the decision.

7. Check for alignment, particularly identifying people who feel they cannot live with the decision. Once the decision is made, stop and ensure that everyone is on board and will act accordingly when they leave the meeting.

8. Identify people who would appreciate knowing what happened in this conversation. Decide how you will inform people who are impacted by the decision and what you need to communicate when you speak with them.

9. Given the decision you made, define what you must do in the next two weeks—what a powerful set of next steps would be, who will take these steps, and by what date. Include these details in the meeting summary.

PROCESS STEPS FOR MAKING A DECISION

- This is the decision we face.
- Who has decision rights?
- How should we decide? What are the objectives and criteria?
- What options do we have?
- What are the benefits and risks of each?
- What is our decision?
- Is everyone OK with this decision?
- How do we communicate this?
- What are the next steps?

5

DESIGN

Creating alignment

Peter Senge defines *alignment* as "what happens when people in a group actually start functioning as a whole." Leaders or groups are likely to seek alignment when defining goals, making decisions, or formulating strategic plans. When it's important to have everyone in the group on board with the outcome, these are the steps to follow to reach alignment:

1. Describe what you would like to do and how you intend to do it. Be clear about your intended outcomes and the path you will use to produce those outcomes.

2. Find out what people are thinking. Start with an open-ended question that allows them to express anything and everything and gives them a chance to direct where the conversation goes. Stay with this conversation as long as they continue to ask questions or offer input.

3. Clarity is often a missing piece, and you want to ask about it directly. Asking whether people are clear gives them permission to say that, for whatever reason, they can't get behind what you are asking.

4. Ask if people see the value in this. People might understand what you are proposing, but if they don't see the value in doing it, they probably won't align.

5. Ask people if they have concerns. People might like your idea, but supporting it might raise a conflict for them. If they can identify their concern, you can determine whether you can address it.

6. Once you know what is in the way, ask whether anything is missing that would make a difference to alignment if it were included.

7. Once you have the items identified in steps 5 and 6, ask the group whether, if you promise to address their concerns and requests, they are now able to align with the decision or plan.

PROCESS STEPS FOR CREATING ALIGNMENT

- Here's what I'd like to do.
- What thoughts or questions do you have?
- Is this clear? Does it make sense?
- Is it worth doing?
- Is there anything in the way of your supporting this?
- Is there anything missing that would help?
- If we address these items, will you align?

More designs and process steps

The process steps in the six designs above are simple and straightforward. In appendix A, you will find tailored design samples as well as additional questions you can use to design the best process steps and questions for your group.

DESIGN

5

One approach to consensus

It's best to avoid voting if you can. Why? Because once people have enough votes, they don't need to listen to the minority. Many organizations have chosen to go with a consensus model, which says consensus is reached if 70 percent of the people support the proposal and 100 percent of the people can live with it.

If someone cannot live with the decision, that person has the responsibility to express the reason. The group then has the responsibility to find a way to address those concerns.

Once resolved, everyone has the responsibility to support the decision. Edgar H. Schein's book *Process Consultation* shares what a team member who would have preferred a different decision, but who chooses to align with the group decision, might say:

> *"I understand what most of you want to do, and I personally would not do that, but I feel that you understand what my alternative would be. I have had sufficient opportunity to sway you to my point of view, but clearly have not been able to do so. Therefore, I will gladly go along with what most of you want to do."*

Closure wraps up the conversation

In a meeting, no topic can be considered complete until it is wrapped up in a thoughtful, deliberate way. There are five elements to effectively closing a conversation: completion, alignment, commitment, value, and appreciation. Not every element of closure must be addressed for each topic, but pulling the conversation together in this way brings a level of clarity about both what happened in the meeting and what will happen next. Closure is also a final opportunity to make sure everyone is aligned and ready to proceed.

Here are the essential elements for closing a conversation:

- **Check for completion:** *Is there anything else to be said or asked?* You don't want people leaving with something unexpressed.

- **Check for alignment:** *Is everyone okay with this?* If someone can't live with the decision or the outcome, ask for what is missing or in the way that, if addressed, would allow the person to align with the group.

- **Confirm commitments:** *What happens next? Who will do what, by when? How and when will we follow up?* Getting firm, clear commitments for action is the primary way to ensure progress.

- **Identify and express value:** *What are we taking away from this conversation?*

- **Express appreciation:** *Did anyone contribute to the conversation in a way that deserves to be highlighted?*

Look for a more complete discussion of closure in the next strategy on leading meetings, pages 134–138.

5

DESIGN

PROCESS STEPS FOR CLOSING A CONVERSATION

Check for completion:

- Is there anything else to be said or asked?

Check for alignment:

- Is everyone OK with where we ended up?
- Is anyone not able to live with this?
- Is there something missing or in the way that, if addressed, would allow you to align?

Check for commitment:

- What happens next?
- Who will do what by when?
- When do we follow up?
- Who will keep track of progress between meetings?

Identify and express value:

- What did we produce?
- What are we taking away from this conversation?

Express appreciation:

- Is there anyone in the meeting we should acknowledge?
- Is there anyone not present who should be acknowledged?

Design matters, regardless of group size or structure

Essentially, the principles of design remain the same regardless of the size of the group or how you are meeting. If you want a conversation to be productive, take the time to be thoughtful about process, whether you're talking with one person or twenty, meeting face-to-face or virtually.

One-on-one meetings deserve design and preparation

For many people, a workweek might consist of fifteen to twenty one-on-one meetings—that's the job. Within our model of a meeting being a series of conversations, one-on-one meetings also deserve careful thinking to design the best way for conversations to be handled.

Most people do not give much thought to preparing for one-on-one meetings, because they know they will be fine if they don't. But being fine isn't the same as being remarkable. A few minutes of preparation will not only enhance how the conversation unfolds, but preparing is a way to show respect for the other person's time. Taking the time to think through how best to have the conversation increases the probability that you will cover both your topic and theirs efficiently.

Let's work within the context of preparing for a meeting with a senior manager in your organization—your immediate supervisor or someone higher in the organization. *Because managers are unlikely to prepare for the meeting, they appreciate it when you do.*

Determine your desired outcomes from the conversation and speculate about theirs. *What do you want them to take away from the conversation? What, if anything, do you want them to do as a result of the conversation?* Then think about how they would answer the same two questions for you.

Think through the best way to conduct the conversation. Then design your introduction or the setup for the meeting. Your setup might sound something like this:

> *"I have two topics I would like to cover. On one of these, I just want to let you know what is happening. On the other, I would appreciate your guidance on how I respond to a*

5

DESIGN

request from another organization. Are there topics that you would like to discuss?"

Then work through each of the topics one by one. When discussing topics you brought to the meeting, express where you stand, and then ask for the manager's thoughts. Discuss the topic in a back-and-forth process until you have what you need.

Finally, at the end of the meeting:

- Clarify what you are taking away from the meeting in terms of understanding and value.

- Explain what you intend to do next and by when.

- Offer to send a quick note capturing the key points, if it makes sense to do so. The topics and your working experience with the person will determine if this is necessary.

If one-on-one meetings are a key part of your workday, taking the time to prepare for meetings with senior managers, colleagues, and employees will be noticed and appreciated.

Consider group size in your meeting design

The flexibility and informality of a group of five generally means there's enough time for each person to speak as often as they want, allowing for a good back-and-forth conversation about each topic. Plus, if people are not clear or have concerns, it's easy for them to speak up.

When you go from five to twenty, the leader needs to be much more deliberate and rigorous about managing the process, which makes having a clear set of process steps critical. Large groups also require more time for discussing a topic to ensure everyone feels heard.

Here are some thoughts for how your design changes when the group is larger:

- You may decide to build in some small-group or breakout conversations to allow time for everyone to express their views or as a way of refining their thoughts before entering the large group conversation.

- Large groups require greater clarity on process steps because the conversation can get sidetracked so easily. A visible way to keep the process steps in front of people (handout, flip chart, whiteboard) helps keep comments on track.

- An agenda sent out ahead of time is even more essential to a group of twenty than a group of five.

- A visible way to capture comments helps keep people from repeating points made earlier.

Meeting design takes on even greater importance when planning conferences or meetings with a hundred or more people. While this book doesn't address the logistics of such endeavors, the basic design principles remain the same.

5

DESIGN

TRY THIS

- ☐ For two weeks, listen for the setup on every topic and assess whether it was adequate.

- ☐ For two weeks, listen for the elements of closure and assess whether the wrap-up for each topic was adequate.

- ☐ Set aside fifteen minutes to prepare for each of your next five one-on-one meetings and see if you notice a qualitative difference in how they work.

Virtual meetings require special consideration

For some managers, almost every meeting is virtual. And while virtual groups increasingly are seeking ways to meet at least occasionally in the same place, global collaboration is only going to continue to expand, along with the need to have conversations in the virtual sphere. So it's important to master this way of working together.

Fortunately, the preparation, design, and leading practices highlighted in this book apply to virtual meetings as directly as they do to face-to-face conversations. Here are twelve points for extra attention when designing, leading, and participating in virtual conversations:

Designing

1. Devote more time to allowing people to connect in the beginning. Relationship-building conversations are more important virtually because people can't get together for coffee. For example, ask a couple of people to share about what is happening where they live.

2. Devote more time for every topic to allow for the deliberate practice of getting people into the conversation.

3. Consider adding a process step to check for clarity on each topic, because without visual cues, you can't always tell if people are understanding or agreeing. If you have people with different cultural or language backgrounds, getting to clarity may require more back-and-forth conversations.

4. Provide not only an agenda but also the process steps for each topic as an aid to keeping people on track.

Leading

5. Have a visible chart on the table in front of you to keep track of who is in the meeting and who has or hasn't spoken. If possible, you might ask someone sitting next to you to track this so you can devote yourself to listening.

6. Use the practice of reflecting comments back to people to verify that you understood what they said. Refer to people by name.

7. Explain the protocol you will use to ensure everyone gets into the conversation. (For example: *"First, I'm going to ask people who are not in the room to begin. Once we've heard from those who are calling in, we'll come back to those of you in the room."*)

8. Call on people. Call on people. Call on people. Make this the norm. It is the only way you can ensure that people feel they have a chance to add value to each conversation. It's also the best way to reduce the amount of multitasking. Just let them know ahead of time and be gentle about it.

9. Get the summary of the meeting out within a few hours and ask for quick confirmation that the details are correct, particularly decisions made, action items, and time lines for completion.

10. Thank people for making the meeting work. Acknowledge the difficulty and stress on families that come with meeting times that, while inconvenient, make it possible for everyone to connect. (You'll find more on leading virtual meetings on pages 142–150 in the next strategy.)

Participating

11. Find a space where it is easy to pay attention to the meeting. No multitasking. If you're in a room with others, resist the urge to have side conversations. Those who are linked in virtually will notice them and feel left out.

12. Speak up if you have any questions about how the meeting will be led or if you aren't clear about anything being said. Don't leave something you need to say or ask unexpressed. State your name each time you speak if you are a remote participant in a group larger than ten.

"When you go to meetings or auditions and you fail to prepare, prepare to fail. It's simple but true."

—Paula Abdul
American singer and songwriter

Lead
Meetings for
Three Outcomes

Core ideas:

- Leading meetings is a core competency for managers.
- Lead the meeting to accomplish the agenda.
  - Get permission to manage the conversation rigorously.
  - Establish agreements to guide the group's interactions.
  - Set up each conversation.
  - Manage conversations so they stay on track.
  - Wrap up each conversation deliberately.
  - Ensure progress between meetings.
  - Be aware of the particular challenges of virtual meetings.
- Lead to create a quality experience for everyone.
  - Take care of people.
  - Refer to people by name.
  - Manage the conversation to balance participation levels.
- Lead to develop new skills and capacity.

"When the best leader's work
is done, the people say,
'We did it ourselves!'"

— Lao-Tsu
Chinese philosopher and poet

Leading meetings is a core competency for managers

A friend and client who is a senior manager in a Fortune 100 company received a promotion that jumped her over people with more experience and more knowledge in the function. Curious, she asked the CEO why she was chosen, and he replied, "Because you are the best person I've ever seen at managing the conversations in a meeting, and at this level, it's all about meetings."

This CEO understood that meetings are at the heart of an effective organization. Each meeting is an opportunity to clarify issues, set direction, sharpen focus, create alignment, and move objectives forward. The ability to make consistent progress in every meeting can be as important as your organizational structure—perhaps more important. *As we flatten organizational structures, set up matrix organizations, and work across the globe, the capacity to lead meetings effectively becomes even more valuable.*

Meetings are too important not to be working to take them to the next level of effectiveness. In fact, meeting skills should be at the heart of every leadership training program.

Organizations often bring in a facilitator to lead important meetings, and for strategic meetings or retreats, this makes sense if expertise does not reside within the group. However, it makes even more sense to build this expertise into the group. All of your meetings would benefit, and the greatest leverage lies in the meetings that happen day in and day out.

The intent of this chapter is to make it possible for you to lead your meetings with the ease and grace of a professional facilitator.

A well-managed conversation isn't necessarily visible. If you love sports, you know the best officiating happens when, after the game is over, you can't remember what the officials did. People should not be left with how well the conversation was led, but with how much got done and how good they feel about having participated.

Of course, if people are not accustomed to excellent meetings, they will notice when your meetings start improving dramatically. That's good, because it raises the bar for all meetings in the organization. Think about the impact if people begin referring to your group's meetings as the way things ought to be done!

6

LEAD

WHAT IF EVERY MEETING...

- is led in a respectful and rigorous way?

- produces the intended results?

- allows everyone to participate and be heard?

- leaves the group more capable of working together?

- sets up the work between meetings powerfully?

Three objectives for leading meetings

Naturally, the first and most important objective is to work through each agenda item and reach the desired outcomes for the meeting. Conducting productive meetings is the cornerstone for all groups who work together. Your first priority is achieving results because not being productive when you meet simply doesn't work.

Second, focus on leading the meeting in a way that encourages and honors the participation of each person. If you do not attend to this aspect of working with others in a group setting, eventually your people will be less engaged, less fulfilled, and less aligned with you and with the organization.

Third, you want to keep getting better at leading meetings, and you want your people to keep getting better at participating. Not only will your meetings improve, but the other meetings your people attend will benefit indirectly. If you are a manager, you might consider it part of your responsibility that your people work on improving their meeting skills each and every year.

The first objective: Lead to accomplish the agenda

The essence of leading an effective meeting includes sharing with your group how you intend to lead it, asking for the permission you need to manage the conversation, and establishing agreements with the group for working together. Then you can deliberately manage the conversation, following the road map developed in the design for the meeting, which outlines the setup, process steps, and closure.

6

LEAD

Get permission to manage the conversation rigorously

Before you begin working on the topics outlined by the agenda, it is important to start your meeting by describing how you intend to lead it. You'll find everything will go more smoothly if you let the group know up front what to expect from you in terms of how the meeting will be led.

People respect well-led meetings. This does not mean highly controlled. It means managing the interaction to create the possibility for thoughtful, deliberate conversation. Good meeting management starts with permission—giving yourself permission and asking for the group's permission to do what is necessary to have a productive conversation.

What would you like the freedom to do as you lead the meeting? What would you like to be able to do and not have to worry about upsetting anyone? You might ask the group's permission to do any of the following:

- Pull the group back if the conversation goes off track.
- Remind the group if distractions get to be an issue.
- Call on people to enrich the conversation.
- Ask for specific commitments for next steps.

You might remind participants that they have permission to do any of the following:

- Ask for clarity at any time.
- Invite others to speak.
- Suggest a change in the process steps.
- Point out when the conversation has gone off track.

By having this conversation before the meeting starts, you graciously ask for the group's support of your managing the conversation.

Establish agreements to guide the group's interactions

Agreements are guidelines you put in place to shape how you interact together. Don Miguel Ruiz made this idea famous with his book, *The Four Agreements*, in which he outlines four paths to personal freedom:

- *Be impeccable with your word.*
- *Don't take anything personally.*
- *Don't make assumptions.*
- *Always do your best.*

In a conversation with a new acquaintance, Rick asked for a couple of ideas from my work that he might use. I discussed the value of establishing agreements in relationships. Rick immediately gave his own compelling example:

My wife is battling cancer, and we made some agreements to guide us as we communicate with each other during these difficult times. Here's what we agreed on together:

- *If she wants to talk about herself, her issues, or her life, I must participate.*
- *If I want to talk about myself or my issues, I must ask her permission.*
- *I promise to remember she is the one who is ill.*
- *She will allow me to contribute to her well-being.*

An agreement is the product of a direct conversation, either when you begin to interact with someone or when you recognize the need for a way to communicate more effectively. Having agreements in place helps avoid common issues and provides a structure within which to solve problems when they do arise.

6

LEAD

In terms of meetings, agreements let people know what behavior is expected and allow participants to say when something doesn't work. Here are three broad and useful agreements for meetings:

1. Please take care of yourself. (If you need to check on something, feel free to step outside and do so.)

2. Ask questions at any time.

3. If something doesn't work, let's talk about it.

These are broad enough to cover almost anything, and the group can ask for clarity, if necessary, to cover specific needs.

Some organizations have created meeting guidelines to remind people of what it means to participate in meetings in a supportive way. These guidelines are established when an organization feels something is missing that would make a difference if it were added.

Focus on what we do best

To give our customers the best products they deserve, we need to focus on what we do best: our core work. By effectively managing our meetings, we will have more time and energy to focus on the needs of our customers.

Please remember these meeting guidelines:

- Respect each other's time: Start on time, follow the agenda, take unrelated topics offline.

- Be fully engaged: Put away phones and laptops.

- Practice effective conversations: Provide clarity, candor, brevity, and closure.

- Keep your word: Capture, share, and follow up on action items.

—Poster at John Deere Waterloo Works

Reprinted with permission.

In strategy 8, on pages 202–203, you will find the set of practices that a group of forty leaders follows. This set provides a good starting place for deciding what agreements might be useful in your group.

An agreement about distraction

Distraction is a big issue these days. Too many of us sit in meetings with a roomful of people consulting laptops, smartphones, or other devices, and this trend needs to be stopped cold in its tracks. Here is how you might express this agreement in the setup for your meeting:

Within the agreement to take care of yourself, you certainly have my permission to leave the room at any time to check on your family or critical projects. I realize you may have calls you are waiting for or projects you are tracking. Do what you need to do to feel you have that handled. Please use your judgment and look out for yourself. You can also get up at any time to get coffee, stretch, use the restroom.

That said, I would love your full attention when we are in the meeting so we can really focus the conversation. So check your electronics at the door. I ask this for two reasons: First, because they are distracting to me and to others. Second, because your attention and listening matter to me, to others in the room, and to the quality of our work together.

If you want to put your phone on vibrate, not a problem, unless it vibrates every five minutes. Exceptions are fine; patterns are troublesome. Also, if you want to take notes or use your tablet to refer to background information on our topics, by all means do so. I just ask that you resist the urge to check e-mail or world news. Deal? Thank you.

6

LEAD

Once you have discussed and agreed upon how the meeting will be conducted, it's time to get to work on the agenda. Using setup, process steps, and closure for each topic on the agenda will allow you to reach your intended outcomes.

Set up each conversation

Setup is about introducing each agenda topic in a way that allows everyone to be at the same starting place, with clarity about what the conversation is intended to achieve and how it will get there.

These are the key elements for setting up a conversation:

- Provide enough background to bring people up to speed and establish the context for the conversation.

- Provide clarity about what you want to produce in the conversation—where you want to be at the end of it and what outcomes you want to achieve.

- Be clear about what you want from people in the meeting—suggestions, feedback, questions, alignment.

- Explain how the conversation will unfold—what the path or process steps will be for getting to the desired outcome.

Often this last piece of setup—explaining the process steps to be followed—is missing, and a group will begin discussing a subject with no outline or plan for working through it. As a result, the conversation jumps all over the place, people begin making the same point over and over, and great points get lost.

This is why conversations deserve to be designed—so there is a clear path to follow in working through a topic.

Let's look at what the setup for a discussion about communicating a new strategic intent document might be:

"We've set aside two hours to discuss how we intend to communicate our new strategic intent document to our stakeholders and employees. You all received the final version earlier this week.

"Today, we'd like to agree on who we need to communicate with and the best way to do that with each group, then assign responsibility for doing so to specific individuals.

"Our intent is first to answer all of your questions about the document, then discuss what our strategic intent makes possible. Then we will develop a list of who we must communicate with and get ideas about how best to do this. Finally, we will identify next steps and make commitments for who will do what by when.

"At the end, we would like everyone to be clear about the process and be excited about moving forward."

Manage conversations so they stay on track

One of the most frequent complaints about meetings is that they take too long, and the main reason for this is conversations are allowed to drift and get off track. Most of us are wired to be caring and supportive. As a perspective and outlook for working with people, this is perfect. If you are the person leading the meeting, however, this should be balanced with a directness that will result in better meetings.

Four primary reasons meetings get off track

First, there's a lack of clarity about the process steps. It's almost as if no track exists. Because most meetings today have not been designed, there is no clear track to follow in working through the conversation. It's easy to go off track onto tangential paths if, before the conversation begins, a track is not made visible with a chart or handout.

Second, some people feel the freedom to say anything at any time but neglect to make sure their comments add value. Or their conversational pattern is to speak often and at length—beyond what is effective.

Third, people love to solve problems, offering ideas and suggestions even when solving a problem isn't the point of the discussion.

Fourth, the person leading the meeting is not comfortable bringing the group back on task even when it's obvious the conversation has strayed. And, while individuals in the meeting may notice the discussion is off track, they usually won't comment unless the group has agreed that this is not only allowed, but requested.

Understand that, as leader of the conversation, you can prevent the discussion from going in a direction that's not productive. Here are some ways you might intervene if the conversation has veered from the intended path:

> *"I'd love to stay with this conversation, but I think we should get back to the agenda."*

> *"It seems to me that we are in a different conversation than we intended; do we want to stay with this new conversation or get back on track?"*

> *"This sounds like an idea we should note and revisit at another time. Is that OK with everyone?"*

I expect the term *off track* came from the world of trains, where derailing isn't what you want a train to do. Conversationally, getting off on an occasional side track won't hurt, but if getting off track becomes a pattern, you are derailing your meetings.

Be careful about PowerPoint or other visual aids

This is very simple: Use technology when it adds to the quality of the conversation. Don't use it if it doesn't.

If visibility can help people follow and participate in a conversation, great. If it doesn't, reconsider its use.

For example, American statistics expert Edward R. Tufte argues that PowerPoint presentations are designed for the presenter, not for the audience. The individual slides are so simplified that they actually stop thinking and listening and encourage distraction.

When Louis Gerstner became president of IBM, he set off a firestorm when he quietly turned off the overhead projector in a presentation by one of his section leaders and said, "Let's just talk about your business."

Bottom line: Does the visual presentation add value to the quality of the conversation?

6

LEAD

Keep track of the conversation visually

The process steps of the meeting design provide a clear track for the conversation to follow. These might be included in the agenda, provided in a handout at the meeting, or written on a whiteboard to be a visible reminder of where you are in the conversation.

Let's take a look at the process steps for a conversation about maintaining the organizational culture in a university leadership group.

Step one: How would you describe our culture?

1. *What do you say about our organizational culture when recruiting new unit leaders (or what would you say)?*

2. *What do you rely upon and like about our way of working together as an organization?*

Step two: What concerns do you have about sustaining our culture?

Step three: Closure

1. *What are you taking away from this conversation?*

2. *What are the next steps?*

The steps and questions above were part of the agenda handed out before the meeting. During the meeting, charting the conversation on a whiteboard helped keep the conversation on track. The illustration below shows how the notes of the conversation about maintaining the organizational culture were later captured in a mind map for the meeting summary.

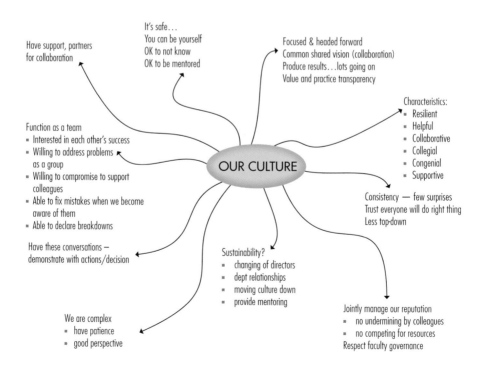

Mind mapping to track conversations

Mind mapping is a powerful visual technique that allows you to capture and quickly recover all of your thinking on a topic. While mind mapping began as a graphical means of thinking visually, it's a useful way to capture the threads of complex conversations.

Since conversations are often free-flowing rather than linear, this form of note-taking can be an advantage.

When used to track a discussion during a meeting, mind mapping gives participants the ability to see what has been said so far and to see how the various themes of a conversation are expressed. Since the mind is not capable of keeping track of more than five to seven things at once, some visual aid is helpful.

The beauty of a mind map is that it is not a list but more of a picture, so it's easy to grasp with just a glance. Plus, new comments can be added where they best fit rather than at the end of your notes on a flip chart.

Begin with the core idea or subject in the center, and as different elements of the idea are defined or expressed, add them around the outside and connect them with a line. Use lines or arrows to link similar ideas or to indicate direction.

6

LEAD

Wrap up each conversation deliberately

By far the most important part of ensuring that a conversation leads to action and progress is being deliberate about wrapping up the conversation. Too many conversations produce ideas and clarity about what actions should be taken only to have nothing get done.

I once kept track of how many times someone in my family brought up an idea for what we might do on the weekend. Nineteen times during the week someone in the family asked to do something or suggested we do something or hinted that we do something. And none of them happened. Why? Because it's easy to talk about doing something; more challenging to pin ourselves down with a commitment.

Good ideas and suggested next steps are often lost due to a lack of closure. Let's go back to the example of the discussion on strategic intent (page 129). Here's what the leader might say in closing this conversation:

> "OK, it seems we've accomplished what we set out to do—we've established our message about what our strategic intent can accomplish and how we need to communicate it. Are there any other comments or questions before we check for alignment and read through the list of next steps?"

> "Good. Is everyone OK with where we ended up?"

> "I'm going to read through the list of commitments we made. Please listen for yours, and if the dates we have listed for your commitments need adjusting, let's get that done now."

> "I'd like to acknowledge the working group who did all the preparation for this meeting. Thank you."

> "Finally, I'd like a few people to share what they are taking away from this conversation. What do you feel good about?"

Check for completion

It's usually wise to check one final time for additional comments or questions. Often people still have something they need to say or ask. If they don't express it, it lingers and takes away from their ability to focus on the next conversation.

"Are there any other questions or comments about this?"

"We're about to change topics, but I want to be sure everyone has had a chance to express any remaining issues or concerns or questions."

Creating alignment

Successful people are always working to have everyone align with new processes, directions, goals, strategic plans, decisions, resource allocations, or organizational changes. They begin new programs and projects by ensuring that everyone is on board. They take whatever time is necessary to talk with and listen to everyone involved. They know that if they spend the time with people initially, there will be fewer conflicts and frustrations later on.

Here is how one of my clients set up a conversation for a meeting to reach alignment:

"Look, I sense that I don't have your support. I may be wrong. Maybe I do have it. Maybe I don't. Maybe I don't deserve it. But let's talk, because I'm unwilling to go ahead without your support."

Check for alignment

For most conversations, a simple *"Is everyone OK with this?"* is sufficient. For major decisions, checking with each person might be in order. Consider who is most affected by the decision, who will be called on to implement it, and who argued for a different decision, then check in with them in a gentle, supportive way to see if they can live with where the group ended up and with what the group intends to do next.

> *"Is everyone agreed on where we ended up on this topic?"*
>
> *"This is an important decision, so I want to be sure I understand where everyone is on it. Do you agree with this option? If not, what's in the way of your alignment or what's missing that might make the difference for you if it were added?"*
>
> *"Is there anyone who can't live with this outcome?"*

Confirm commitments

Certainly, determining the next steps and actions is the most important step because it is the best way to ensure that something happens after the meeting. If you are specific when you ask someone to do something, and if you ask for it to be done by a specific date, it is more likely to happen. Think of a commitment as **who** is going to do **what** (X) by **when** (Y). People usually get the first two pieces committed but leave out the "by when." If you can get "X by Y" to be the norm in your group, you will get more accomplished. If you do nothing else, get these actions noted and agreed upon.

Identify and express value

One of the most powerful acknowledgment tools is to express what value you are taking away from a conversation. Doing so not only communicates what you got out of the discussion, it acknowledges the other people participating in it.

The most obvious accomplishment of a meeting is to agree upon decisions made and actions to be taken. But sometimes simply the process of having a long, intense conversation generates other kinds of value. People appreciate an opportunity to express what they are taking away from the conversation. As the leader, invite three to four people to share what they are taking away from the meeting, then add a couple of expressions of value for yourself.

> *"I'm leaving this meeting with a sense that we are going to do something, and I appreciate the commitments people have made."*

> *"I'm taking away clarity about the decision process that I can explain to people who work in my area."*

Express appreciation

Letting people know you appreciate them is something that's often missing in organizations. Reflect on the conversation and see if someone, present or not, deserves acknowledgment for what they provided to the discussion or what they have done outside of the meeting room.

> *"Cheryl, I appreciate that you questioned whether we were doing enough on the issue of employee engagement. Your comment changed the entire conversation for me."*

> *"Mark, you and a couple of others referred to the wonderful support you have been getting from information systems. Would you let them know that our group appreciates what they do?"*

> *"Juan, here's what your comments made me realize about the work we've taken on."*

Bottom line: If you stop reading this book right now and spend the next three weeks closing every conversation in a deliberate, thoughtful way, you would see immediate shifts in what gets done. This extends way beyond meetings. As a manager or supervisor, if you take time for this process step whenever someone meets with you one-on-one, the conversation and what happens as a result will shift dramatically.

Value—the missing piece

While providing a leadership workshop for Dave in the Netherlands, a previous client, Aaron, stopped by for a factory visit. Aaron was at this time the worldwide business leader for the product line produced at the factory. As with many VIP visits, a morning was set aside for young people to make a series of presentations to Dave and Aaron. I had the opportunity to sit in and listen. At the end of the first presentation, Aaron thanked the young man for the presentation and told him he had done well.

At that point, I stepped in and reminded Aaron of a key piece of closing a conversation—expressing value. Aaron, who was already beyond good before I met him, quickly agreed and backtracked. He then shared four distinct things that he was taking away from the young man's presentation.

When you wrap up a conversation by sharing something you are taking away from it, you validate not only the conversation, but the other person involved in it. Plus, if you know you plan to express value at the end, you will listen for and actually see more value!

Credit for this idea doesn't belong to me. In fact, I could call it the Evans Protocol, after a client and friend at Oregon State University, Gwil Evans, whose practice of noticing and expressing value from conversations extends from formal meetings to casual gatherings over coffee. As you can imagine, people loved being in meetings designed and led by Gwil.

Ensure progress between meetings

"Prayer without action is the same thing as no prayer at all."
—Mother Teresa

No matter how productive a meeting seems, what happens after the meeting is over is more important. If you do not keep the commitments that are generated during the meeting, not only will you not make progress, but it is discouraging to members of the group to start the next meeting with a lack of progress. Lack of follow-up and little or no documentation of what was discussed and decided are two of the most common reasons that meetings fail to deliver on expectations.

Being able to represent what happened in a meeting to people who might be interested is also something to be thoughtful about after each meeting. Progress is aided by having people who don't attend the meeting informed and included.

Follow up

There's a lot of value that occurs in conversation: finding clarity, reaching alignment, creating a shared understanding of what matters. The piece to have your eye on continually, however, is what will happen as a result of the meeting? We've all left meetings feeling good about what was discussed only to end up later wondering why so little happened as a result.

Good meetings and good intentions are not enough to ensure the work that is produced during a meeting continues once the meeting is over. For example, a university president asked me to provide some

6

LEAD

leadership training for the university. I asked him why he thought such training was necessary.

"Well, two years ago I pulled together a group of faculty and alumni to discuss starting a new school of journalism. We had a wonderful meeting, and everyone was excited about making it happen. I told them I was willing and available to provide whatever support they might need. I left the meeting feeling very positive about getting that new school started. Two years later, nothing has happened because no one in that meeting had any leadership skills."

I responded with, "Actually, you don't have a new school because you didn't follow up. If you'd checked in with the group two weeks after the meeting, then followed up every few weeks until the project was up and running, you'd have your journalism school."

If you want anything in life to happen, you must follow up, follow up, and follow up. Persistence is a key influence skill.

Good managers get caught up in thinking that people are self-starters —natural leaders who only need an idea and the autonomy to pursue it. But people are busy. They have so many commitments pulling at them. Rich ideas fall by the wayside easily because no one is sitting around with eight or twelve free hours for starting a new project.

Some managers are also concerned that close follow-up might be interpreted as micromanaging. They don't want to be accused of not trusting people to perform. In reality, consistent follow-up is just good project leadership.

A written summary keeps the conversation alive

> "The palest ink is better than the best memory."
> —Chinese proverb

Historically, minutes were like court transcriptions, capturing everything that was said during the meeting. That is not what you want. Ideally, meeting summaries keep your discussions, decisions, and actions alive and working after the meeting is over. In particular, they remind everyone of the commitments that were made, which is essential to getting the required work done before the next meeting.

A single page will suffice for most meetings. The intent here is not to re-create the discussions but to capture the key points and the specific commitments made for each topic, so that non-attendees have some sense of what happened and all have a record of who will take further action.

Write and distribute the meeting summary within twenty-four hours, if not sooner. Your ability to remember and capture the essence of each conversation lessens with each passing hour.

Since conversation vanishes quickly, the write-up of a meeting determines how it will persist and extend influence beyond the actual meeting. It is because conversations disappear that you often end up having the same conversation over and over. Sometimes this repetition happens when someone who couldn't make it to the last meeting asks that the previous meeting be re-created for them. The summary provides a place for people to get in touch with what was discussed, the key points in each conversation, and the actions agreed upon.

6

LEAD

If you work to narrow the number of people invited to a meeting, the summary takes on more importance because people love to be included and informed. Be thoughtful about who does not attend and how best to include and take care of them. Sharing a summary of the meeting can be an important part of that effort.

Be aware of the particular challenges of virtual meetings

With the globalization of business, virtual meetings are becoming the norm for many conversations. Video conferencing technology has made it possible for virtual meetings to include many elements of face-to-face meetings. Still, not being present in the same room creates challenges to overcome if your meetings are going to be effective.

Lynn Haeffele, a hardware supply manager for a major high-tech company, has been leading virtual meetings with global partners for more than fifteen years, and she shared her insights in a recent interview. I was delighted with how thoroughly our ideas mesh on designing and leading meetings.

Lynn Haeffele on dealing with the challenges of meeting virtually

The virtual meeting is the hardest meeting environment; it's the hardest environment in which to get your point across. But you need to be aware that it's a challenge, and then look for ways to be creative in rising to that challenge.

One of the biggest challenges with meetings that are not face-to-face is that you can be assured people are not really focused on you. They're looking at e-mail, they're getting instant messages, they're sending texts. They're behind on everything, and the temptation to take care of that instead of being attentive in the meeting is huge.

So for my part, extra preparation is key. I do as much home-work up front because the attention span in a virtual meeting is a fraction of what it is in face-to-face meetings.

I was helping out in a school classroom once, and the children were having difficulty with the concept of telling time. The teacher asked me to take them to a separate room, where I explained in great detail the various elements required to tell time. They still weren't getting it. So I ramped up the speed at which I delivered the information, and suddenly they got it. If you move slowly, you lose people. You've got to keep things snappy.

I always have something visual that marks where we are in the meeting. I'll have something on the virtual shared screen, typically the agenda or an action item tracker. I always track relevant meeting conversations and decisions because I know that in six months, I may need to refer back to them.

I always ask people by name to respond to the discussion. I used to get a lot of, "Oh, I'm sorry, I didn't get that. I was multitasking." But it doesn't happen anymore. They know I'm going to call on them, and they need to be paying attention.

Engaging people

Before the meeting starts, I like to engage people in personal conversations—how's the weather, what did you do with your time off, what's new in your city, inundating them with news of my granddaughter, and so forth. Part of this is getting people to participate and stay engaged in the conversation. Part of it is making sure they know you care, and if you've taken the time to develop that sense of caring and respect, then they're more likely to respond in kind.

6

LEAD

It's easy to jump right into the action list because you know you have so much to cover in a limited amount of time, but it's critical to engage your meeting attendees up front because then they're much more likely to stay engaged for the meeting.

I like to sprinkle light humor throughout the meeting—putting someone's off-the-cuff remark in the notes and reading it aloud—it's part of reminding people to stay engaged.

It takes me probably four times as much energy to run a virtual meeting as it does for a face-to-face meeting. Your voice has to capture their interest; it's a tool to keep people engaged. It's what you have to use in the absence of body language and facial expressions to express delight, passion, enthusiasm. It's a challenge!

One of the things that happened in the beginning was I would jump into meetings from where I was. I wasn't taking into account that no one else knew my frame of reference or had my backstory. So going into a meeting now, I allow time to bring people up to my knowledge base—I give them the backstory to get us to the starting line together. Then I start the meeting.

Tracking accountability

During the meeting, I often keep an action-item tracker on screen. For example, I have one meeting that happens every week. What's on the screen is what we have to cover, along with notes on what was decided at last week's meeting. It includes the action items assigned the previous week. Before the meeting, I send this list to all the principals as a reminder, so they can be prepared or get the action done before the meeting. (Helps eliminate "I forgot.") All this grew out of my need to keep track of the ongoing discussions—I couldn't remember from week to week, so I developed a tool for myself, but it's become a really valuable tool for running the meeting—you can't hold people accountable without something like this.

Keeping the meeting on track

During the meeting, I'll take a pulse frequently to gauge where people are with a discussion, how much time we've taken for the agenda items thus far, and how much we still need to cover. If we've covered only three items and there are eight left and only twenty more minutes to the meeting, we'll often set some of these discussions as offline meetings rather than extend this meeting.

So that becomes an action item for the next week: Set meeting with X, Y, and Z to cover A, B, and C. And at the next meeting, it will be on the action tracker for us to check in about.

It's very easy to get off in the bushes, especially when you've worked to create an environment that's informal and friendly to keep people engaged. So I'm constantly having to corral people back so we can stay on task and finish the agenda.

Always it's my goal to finish meetings early. If you have meetings that consistently run over, you lose people.

If we're falling behind, I take a pulse: We can opt to table a discussion until the end of the meeting, and if people want to stay and finish, fine; or we can schedule another meeting. Often people would rather take another ten minutes to finish a discussion than have to schedule another meeting, even if it means being late to the next meeting (seems everyone is always scheduled back-to-back).

6

LEAD

Understanding global/cultural issues

There is no good meeting time for a team that consists of people in the United States, Europe, China, India, and South America. We worked it out by alternating meeting times, so it's a little painful for everyone part of the time—sharing the pain.

Often the tools you use don't translate well across cultures: humor is one; timing is another. Another cultural difference is that not everyone shares the same sense of urgency that is typical in American corporations. We work at high speed, in general, and the turnaround expectation is high. And the need for precision in one's instructions varies.

During his last show, Conan O'Brien told the audience not to be cynical—that anything is possible with kindness and hard work. And that's something that crosses cultural boundaries: kindness and hard work. That translates—even through the phone.

Bringing in new people

I'm not one for contrived icebreakers. I think they're artificial and meaningless and do nothing to move a meeting forward. Typically, if we're on a call and no one has met, I'll have people do quick roundtable introductions, talking about themselves and what they do.

I engage people in the discussion by name both to get their input and to let them know that I value their contributions. I used to be a bit like a bull in a china shop, so I had to develop some finesse. When I started, I took virtual meetings too seriously. They can be playful and fun and still be productive.

—Lynn Haeffele,
Hardware Supply Manager for a Fortune 50 company

Agreements for virtual groups

One aspect of working globally and virtually is being more deliberate and clear about how a group will work together both during conference calls and between conference calls. I worked with a worldwide manufacturing team that, for a variety of reasons, simply could not budget the time or money to meet face-to-face, even once. The group leader, reflecting upon the success of the group, referred to the time we spent up front helping the group get to know each other and then establishing a set of guidelines for working together.

One simple answer to questions about working virtually is to be both transparent and explicit about how the group will work together, then find a way for everyone to remain conscious of these agreements.

Having agreements in place provides a critical structure within which to communicate in virtual meetings. You will notice that the agreements this group established, reprinted here, would be just as useful to a group that does have the luxury of meeting face-to-face.

6

LEAD

Worldwide Manufacturing Team Agreements

Since much of our communication will be conducted by conference call, it is essential that we follow these guidelines:

- When someone is speaking, each of us listens fully to understand what each individual is trying to communicate.

- If we don't understand or we disagree, it is each person's obligation to say so. It is impossible to visually assess whether or not there is understanding or concern, so each of us needs to express it.

- For our conference calls, we will ask for an acknowledgment of understanding and/or acceptance by every participating team member for each major point or issue discussed. This will help assure that everyone knows everyone else's position before we move on to other topics.

- We will create an environment for our team where we feel comfortable making very specific requests of one another for information, for help, etc. In other words, if we want something specific, ask for what we want and when we want it by. It is also OK to say no to a request or to offer a modification so we can make commitments that work in response to requests.

- Once a commitment is made, we honor it; if we are unable to meet the commitment, we make contact and renegotiate. Note: It is OK to fail to meet all commitments we make, but it is not OK to neglect to communicate that we won't be able to deliver on time prior to the commitment date.

- Because we will not always be able to have 100 percent participation, we need to consider the questions or concerns those unable to attend may have and do our best to speak for those who are absent. Still, if you are unable to attend, it is your obligation to ask another team member to represent you.

- Although we may not always be able to get 100 percent agreement on what we need to do, it is critical that we have 100 percent alignment. We will acknowledge those areas (and also document them as part of the notes) where we don't have 100 percent agreement, but once we as a team commit to an activity or path forward, the entire team will be aligned on that activity or path.

- Let's acknowledge and appreciate each other. We have a team that can drive real progress in areas that will significantly impact the success of the organization. An important ingredient in making this team's work a positive and rewarding experience for each of us is consistently acknowledging and appreciating one another.

Bottom line: Virtual meetings and global teams can be just as powerful as meetings and teams that are not constrained by geography. It just takes the intention to make them remarkable and more time talking about how people will talk and work together.

The question of cultural differences

Cultural differences exist, and if you want to be great in the world, be open to increasing your awareness of these differences.

Here, however, I want to make a point about the differences that exist between individuals regardless of cultural background, because these tend to get overlooked. We are each unique expressions of not only our culture, but our gender, our families, our experiences, our education, our personalities, our age, our conversational preferences, and the conversations in which we were raised. We are not enough alike to be put in boxes or accurately labeled by any stereotypical expression, such as *engineers are like this, women are like this, Germans are like this.*

> *"It's safe to make just one generalization about India — which is that every other time you generalize about India, you're probably wrong. With over 400 living languages, 85 political parties and a 5,000-year-old cultural and intellectual history, India is defined by its heterogeneity."*
>
> —Payal Sampat, *World Watch Magazine*

We do have amazing levels of common ground—we care about our families, we want to contribute, we want to belong, we want to be respected, we want to live life in a fulfilling way. There is a lot that binds us in powerful ways.

My friend Larry Roper says it more eloquently: "When we create space for another's voice and their story, we honor the core of who they are. While the texture of individual stories and the voice in which one's hopes, expectations, and needs vary, the request to be heard, cared about, and valued is universal. When we become great listeners, we heighten our cultural competency and our ability to create space for cultural diversity."

6

LEAD

The intent of this book is to find a common way of interacting with one another in meetings that does not require us to become proficient in the nuances of every culture. If we can converse and work together with open minds and good intentions, that will carry us past whatever boundaries exist, real or imagined.

Here are some thoughts to consider:

- Everyone is unique.

- We don't know another person's reality or their story.

- Appreciating the differences among individuals can provide helpful hints in being better citizens of the world.

- Giving people permission to give you feedback about their culture is a powerful demonstration of openness.

- If we get to know each other, then mistakes will simply be mistakes rather than events that make us feel separate.

We should take advantage of every opportunity to learn about one another—set aside time to go to coffee, share a meal, take a walk. We honor someone else's story when we make the effort to learn more.

My hope is that the contents of this book will provide guidance for building an understanding and multicultural organization. Paying attention to participation patterns, asking for requests, listening deeply, and following through represent the hallmarks of cultural sensitivity.

The inclusive organization we seek and the skills required to build such an organization are achieved through a conversational style that respects and includes everybody.

6

LEAD

The second objective: Lead to create a quality experience for everyone

When I ask people to reflect on their experience of being in a group, two themes emerge. First, they comment about whether they feel welcome, whether they belong, and whether people in the meeting seem interested in them as people. Second, they comment on whether they feel as if their comments are heard and add value.

The first theme—feeling as if you are a part of the group—is addressed in strategies 2 and 3. Let's focus here on what allows people to leave a meeting feeling as if they have contributed something of value and were heard. The intent is for your meeting to feel like a small group of friends having coffee while being exceptionally productive.

Take care of people

It's not that people need to be looked after. It's simply what works. Taking care of people begins with listening. This is how you, as the person leading the conversation, take care of people when they speak:

- Devote your attention to them while they are speaking.
- Be sure they have the attention of the group.
- Let them finish without interruption.
- Acknowledge that you understand what they said; summarize, if necessary.
- If unclear, stay in the conversation with them until clarity is reached.
- Ask, *"Is there anything else?"* to check whether they have finished.
- Consider and respond to what they say.
- Link their comments to the topic to make the connection clear and to show the value added to the conversation.

6

LEAD

This is why leading a meeting is hard work! To pay attention to each person and then make what they say add value is as challenging as it is rewarding in the end. Consider this view: *It's your job, not theirs, to make sure what each participant says adds value.* Of course, this isn't always true, but it's a powerful perspective to adopt when leading meetings. Part of pursuing mastery is to take ownership for everything in the meeting.

Refer to people by name

It's both polite and reinforcing to let people know when something they said influenced your thinking. By referring to someone's comments, you acknowledge both the person and the value added to the conversation.

> *"I'd like to build on the idea that Sarah introduced."*
>
> *"Jim's comments made me reconsider what I said earlier."*
>
> *"I appreciate what Mark said. It makes me realize what people in operations have been dealing with in the last few weeks."*

Manage the conversation to balance participation levels

You can make an exponential difference in the success of your meetings by managing the way people participate in the conversation. Doing so is important for these reasons:

- You want each person to leave the meeting with the feeling of having contributed their thinking and having been heard.

- Getting more perspectives into the discussion increases the richness of the conversation and the creativity of the group.

- The outcomes and the degree of alignment for those outcomes improves with broad participation.

- A few people dominating the conversation lessens the experience for others.
- People want to feel good about being part of a group, and the best way is to add value to the discussion.

There are two ways to balance participation levels in meetings:

1. Invite people to speak—call on them directly.
2. Be deliberate about managing who speaks—when and how often they speak.

Inviting people to speak

Part of creating an effective group conversation is establishing broad participation. Most people have something to add—if you invite them to speak. Each person has a unique set of perspectives, experiences, and interests, but if they don't share them, you miss out on the value they could add. People get value from attending meetings and listening to the discussions, but they can't contribute if they don't speak. **Many people will not speak if you leave it completely up to them.** But, if you don't get everyone included in the conversation, someone might leave feeling he or she had something to add, but no one was interested in hearing it.

One of the most valuable—and most absent—ways to change the pattern of not speaking is by calling on people and inviting them into the conversation. The key word is *invite*. It creates a perspective of inclusion and gentleness. When you think of inviting someone to speak, your tone of voice will reflect that your intention is to be inviting, not commanding. You're not putting people on the spot but inviting them into the conversation because you want to hear what they have to say. Inviting people to speak provides a number of advantages. Doing so:

- changes the dynamic of the group's normal process,
- adds new thinking and perspectives,

- improves everyone's experience of being in the group,
- changes how people listen and pay attention,
- indirectly trains others to speak more or speak less,
- demonstrates that the conversation is being deliberately managed,
- reduces the tendency to multitask, and
- increases alignment with group decisions.

Those who lead meetings choose not to call on people for a variety of reasons. Some argue it creates an environment that can feel unsafe or that it makes some people so uncomfortable they dread coming to your meetings. However, if you say up front that you plan to manage the conversation by asking people to speak, you will find it easier to call on people, and they will understand your intention when you do. Be sure to let people know that if they don't have anything to add, they can say so—you are simply inviting them to add to the conversation.

I am not talking about random, arbitrary, pull-someone's-name-out-of-the-hat calling on people. I am talking about thoughtfully and deliberately calling on individuals when the conversation would be enhanced by their contributions.

There are other reasons you might invite certain people into the conversation to add to the topic at hand. Maybe you have people with organizational history who can tell you something you should be aware of so you don't repeat mistakes made in the past. Maybe some veteran employees tend not to get into the conversation, but they would be good people to check with to see if they have anything to add.

Call on people to enrich the conversation, and only if you authentically want to hear their views on a topic. Never call on people to put them on the spot. For example, if you notice they are multitasking, do not call on them to get their attention. *You always want people to feel good about being called upon to share their views.*

Todd, a workforce initiatives manager for a community college who had participated in a seminar on meetings, wrote about taking the idea of calling on people back to his meetings: "I have intentionally focused on calling on people *strategically and gently*—perhaps those who are quiet or seem frustrated. . . . It's like magic—an awesome tool."

When inviting someone to speak, your tone of voice needs to indicate this is an invitation, but it's important to be direct as well.

> *"I want to hear from some people who haven't been in the conversation yet. Cindy, William, Chandra—you haven't been heard yet. I want to check in with you to see if you have any questions or comments. Then I'll come back to Damon and Inez, who have indicated they have something to add."*

> *"I want to be sure that anyone who hasn't spoken yet or who spoke earlier and has additional comments can voice them."*

Why people don't speak

I always felt that if I did everything possible to make it easy for people to express themselves, they would participate. I was wrong. You cannot count on people speaking up in a meeting, and I can think of several reasons they don't:

- Their personal conversational style is reflective and quiet.

- Others jump in so quickly, they get left out.

- The meetings tend to run over, so the sense of time gets in the way.

- The person leading the meeting speaks too much.

- They have gentle, subtle ways of trying to get into the conversation that are easily overlooked.

- They're uncomfortable because they don't know many people in the meeting or the group feels too large or the boss is there.

- They had a bad previous experience related to speaking up.

A few years ago, I was leading a strategic planning retreat for senior managers in an organization. At the first break, one of the participants came up and made a very unusual request.

"Paul, I need you to call on me."

I immediately apologized for not conducting the session in a way that allowed her to get into the conversation.

"No, you're doing just fine, and I need you to call on me."

I replied that I would, and I would also appreciate understanding why she was asking.

"Well, I realize I should be over this by now, but every time I think I've got something to say, I can hear my father talking to me. When I was small, every time I said something, he would tell me that I was backward. I've tried to get past it, but now I just accept it and ask people to call on me."

Wow. Here was this bright, polished senior executive who was intent on not letting this one aspect of her past determine her future.

For the rest of the retreat, I made it a point to call on her, and while sometimes she would pass, usually she had something brilliant to add to the conversation.

I learned my lesson. It doesn't matter why people tend to be quiet. The point is, to have truly effective group conversations, you want to ensure that everyone who has something to say has the opportunity to be heard. The surest way to do that is to call on people directly. Given the importance of meetings, it's time to get over the fear of putting people on the spot and simply invite them to speak.

Is it OK if people don't speak? It may not make sense to get every person in the meeting involved in every conversation. First, there may not be enough time. Second, you do want to honor people's conversational preferences. Balancing participation levels doesn't mean everyone should speak the same amount. Topics differ, and what you want from the group or what each person can contribute to the topic will vary from meeting to meeting.

And while I usually argue that people don't provide value to a meeting unless they speak, when they pay attention to the conversation and then readily take on work, that's an impactful way to add value. Being present in the meeting also provides the background understanding they need to do the work in accordance with the group's thinking.

Improving group patterns

You might also call on people to shift the normal ways they participate. If you don't call on people, you are likely to see the same pattern in every meeting. Mary speaks first, Susan speaks second, John speaks third, Renee always waits till the end of the topic and then she joins in. Randy and Ricardo never speak. The patterns repeat time after time, influencing how people participate, whether they participate, and sometimes overly influencing the topic or outcome.

If you are deliberate about changing the pattern from time to time or based on the agenda topic, it will most likely improve the quality of your conversations and the experience of people attending.

Ensuring alignment

It is particularly important to call on people when you are looking for alignment. You want to be sure the place you end up in the conversation is carried out into the organization in a consistent manner.

Consider the people who would be most affected by the decision you will make as a result of this meeting. You want them aligned with the decision, but if you don't ask for their input, that alignment is less assured.

Reaching alignment requires deliberately checking in with people to see if they are able to support the decision of the group. Sometimes people come into a meeting not aligned with where the group is. The only way for them to hold on to that position is to say nothing. In a sense, they get stuck with their own thinking, yet if you can get them into the conversation and then listen to them in an authentic way, you give them the opening they need to change their mind. Getting people to act and speak consistently with the thinking or the decision of the group is one of the fundamental reasons we meet.

Intervening when people speak more than they should

Calling on people is one part of balancing participation levels. Another key practice is to deliberately manage when and how long people speak. In an hour-long meeting of ten people, everyone, on average, gets six minutes. If some people tend to speak more often or longer than they should, eventually their speaking has less impact and they lose the respect of the group. At some point, the group also expects the person managing the meeting to do something about the person dominating the conversation.

How do you manage people who speak too often or beyond the point of adding value? How do you make them aware of what they are doing and of the impact it has on the group as a whole? You must handle this situation in a way that the people watching you can respect. This is where establishing permission at the beginning of the meeting to manage the conversation rigorously is essential. This allows you to intervene when you see it is necessary to ensure you can complete the topic in the time allowed and leave time for others to add their views.

Let's talk about how you handle it in the moment. Your objective is simply to improve the conversation's efficiency rather than changing the person involved. The first time someone speaks too much or too long, you do nothing; you listen thoroughly, without interrupting, so the group knows you are willing to listen and treat this person's conversation—every word—as if it matters.

You might even do this a second time. But by the third time, you want to change the pattern. For example, you could say, *"Laura, if you don't mind, I would like to interrupt for a moment to get some other people into the conversation. But make sure I check back with you to see if something hasn't been said that you would like to add."*

In this case, you acknowledge that Laura wants to add to the conversation, and you simply ask her to wait until you get some other viewpoints.

Bottom line: The attention you put on managing people's experience of your meetings will also improve the results of your meetings over time.

The third objective: Lead to develop new skills and capacity

Each meeting provides an opportunity to get better at leading and participating in meetings. There are a number of ways to lead the meeting so you improve not only your skills, but the skills of the group.

Be deliberate about what you are doing; tell them what you are working on. It's a powerful testament to learning as a lifetime occupation.

6

LEAD

"I'm working on keeping my meetings on track. So please excuse me if I seem to be jumping in too quickly to bring you back."

"I'm going to be deliberate about each step in closing our conversations today. I don't feel I do that well, and with your support, I'm going to take a few extra minutes doing that today."

You can also ask people to work on a part of the process in each meeting. You might ask for their help in keeping the conversations on track. Maybe ask them to invite other people into the conversation if they notice someone who hasn't spoken yet or who is looking to contribute. If you ask people to observe for a particular process piece, they will begin to recognize when it's missing and provide it.

In the interest of developing organizational skill around leading meetings, you might ask different members of your group to facilitate a single topic in the meeting or perhaps the full meeting.

Ask someone to observe you as you lead the meeting with the intention of giving you feedback. This is valuable for two reasons: First, you will be better simply because you are being watched. Second, someone observing will be able to give you insights on your performance and build his or her own awareness. See "Observing Meetings," in appendix D, page 329.

Assign roles to people in larger meetings where your attention will be on managing the conversation. You might ask someone to chart the discussion for you, to watch for who hasn't spoken up yet, to keep track of the commitments made, or to take notes to support writing the summary of the meeting.

By leading one effective meeting after another, you become a role model for how it's done, and people will learn by watching you.

Focus on critical variables

Focus on the critical variables around meetings that will have the most impact on keeping your meetings productive. The entire list in the "TRY THIS" box below is about process—the "how" of working on something. As you learn more about process during meetings, your capability and capacity to be effective will improve in all of your conversations.

The notion of this book ending up "dog-eared" applies here. There are many ideas associated with leading meetings that can be practiced and mastered. Yet if you want a quick way to get started, the short list of critical variables in the "TRY THIS" box is where to put your focus for the next two weeks. You'll soon begin to notice what's missing, and when you notice, you can choose to provide it.

6

LEAD

TRY THIS

☐ Focus on critical variables for the setup:
- Have you established permission to lead and agreements for the group? Do people know they can say or ask anything?
- Are the outcomes for each conversation clear?
- Is the process to be followed clear?

☐ Focus on critical variables for managing the conversation:
- Has the conversation veered off track?
- Has each conversation been taken to completion with next steps identified?
- Was everyone taken care of during the conversation?

Two final thoughts for leading meetings

Be present

In a context where meetings matter, it's important to get into a space where you are ready to lead the meeting. Don't rush in at the last minute. Get the room set up early, get some coffee or water, relax, and prepare to lead.

> *"Horowitz came out on stage to a standing ovation. Then he just sat there for a while and gazed into the audience. As everyone settled down, you could tell that he was also settling down; letting all the emotions, all the nerves, all the political implications subside in his mind so that mastery could emerge, and his hands would perform what they had been trained to do so well. Watching him unburden himself in this way was electrifying for me, because I understood what he was doing."*
>
> —Kenny Werner, *Effortless Mastery*

This quote pushes the envelope, for sure. It is about performing and presence—not things we normally think about in the context of meetings. But why not? We want to raise the bar dramatically on the art and possibility associated with leading meetings.

Taking time to pause—even for a few moments—will add to your ability to be present both before and during the meeting. People will respond to your way of being as the meeting begins. You can focus on being calm and calming, relaxed and light, engaged and intentional—whatever seems to fit you and the group and the meeting.

Be yourself at your best

> *"Kindergarten teachers often understand the craft better than those of us with Ph.D.'s, perhaps because students in the lower grades are like the child in ' The Emperor's New Clothes.' They quickly sense whether you are real, and they respond accordingly."*
>
> —Parker Palmer, *The Courage to Teach*

It all starts with you. People want to work with people they like and respect. You've got to be good. Not perfect or amazing. Just good. Your credibility and reputation, in and out of the meeting room, are critical. You want to be someone who deals with life and the world in a way people admire. You want to be someone who can connect quickly—the kind of person people want to be around. You want to have credibility in the organization for producing results and being easy to work with. And you've got to be real—which is simply yourself at your best.

Bottom line: Be yourself. As Oscar Wilde famously said, "Everyone else is already taken."

6

LEAD

"It is our choices, Harry,
that show what we truly are,
far more than our abilities."

—Albus Dumbledore in J.K. Rowling's
Harry Potter and the Chamber of Secrets

Participate
in Meetings
to Have Impact

Core ideas:

- Choose ownership for each meeting: perspective shapes your participation.

- Practice focused listening: be attentive, patient, nonjudgmental, and listening for something new.

- Practice focused speaking: be clear, concise, relevant, and respectful.

- Participate in ways that add impact: support the person leading the meeting, look out for other participants, ask for what you need, and practice self-awareness.

"If there is an experience
in front of you,
have it."

—Banana Republic advertisement

Choose ownership for each meeting

Most of us walk into meetings concerned about one person—ourselves. We're not usually looking out for other participants or thinking about how to support the person leading the meeting. We sit where we feel most comfortable, and we speak when we feel like it or not at all.

Looking out for ourselves is normal and will always be part of who we are. Still, as a perspective, it dooms us to being less than brilliant—to squandering the value we might add.

On the other hand, if we walk into meetings with a focus on supporting others and doing whatever we can to ensure the meeting turns out well, we will see opportunities to do both.

> WHAT IF...
>
> - You took responsibility for every meeting you attend?
>
> - You knew that others valued your contributions?

Perspective shapes your participation

The mindset you have when you come into a meeting determines how you participate. In many organizations, people have become complacent about the meetings they attend. Unless it's their meeting, they don't prepare or participate in an effective way. Simply changing that mindset would do wonders.

Disengaged is not an option

My friend Alice shared this story:

I was being coached for the first time, and I told Jan how a meeting had "gone bad" and I had pushed back from the table and disengaged. Jan very firmly told me I was not allowed to do that and asked me to come up with some alternate strategies. It was some of the most helpful thinking I ever received about meetings—that staying engaged and interested was required, not optional.

Alice's initial response is typical. A more effective response when a meeting stops working is to set that first reaction aside and find a way to move forward. You will feel better if you act in a way that is consistent with your own values and standards for participating in life.

Too often we put our attention on looking for evidence that we are right about a particular person or situation. It might be time to realize this doesn't work out in the long run.

7

PARTICIPATE

You are the only person in the meeting with your experience, expertise, interests, concerns, and point of view. If you don't share your thinking, the group misses out.

I've always loved the story about three kinds of people—the ones who make things happen, the ones who watch things happen, and the ones who wonder what happened. Being on the sidelines in life is interesting, but other than when supporting our kids at their soccer games, it doesn't add much value.

There is a fundamental difference between experiencing life directly and watching it from a distance. Far better to choose to participate in a way that allows you to contribute.

One of my favorite stories is from anthropologist and visionary Loren Eiseley about encountering a young man on the beach picking up stranded starfish one by one and throwing them back into the ocean. Eventually the author questions the young man's sanity because there are stranded starfish as far as the eye could see. The young man smiles, picks up another starfish and throws it back. "Made a difference to that one!"

The choice is yours. You can either sit on the sidelines, wishing the meeting were over, or listen for what you might do to support the leader and other participants.

Practice focused listening

> "An example of a system well managed is an orchestra.
> The various players are not there as prima donnas—
> to play loud and attract the attention of the listener....
> In fact, sometimes you see a whole section doing nothing
> but counting and watching.... They're there to support
> each other. That's how business should be."
>
> —W. Edwards Deming, American engineer, statistician,
> and management consultant

One's experience of being in a group setting is determined by many things. One of them is, *Do I have an opportunity to share my thoughts, and when I do, are people listening?* This might not be a missing piece for you, but it is likely to be a concern for someone in your group. The way you listen to each person has an impact.

Focused listening has four components: paying attention, having patience, being nonjudgmental, and choosing to listen for something in particular in every meeting.

The first component: Be attentive

The Edwards Deming quote is about paying attention. It's about avoiding distracting or disinterested behavior when someone else is speaking. Doing nothing—and staying engaged.

How do you do this? Leave your technology at the door. Keep only what you need for the meeting in front of you. Sit in a way that conveys interest; your posture and other types of nonverbal communication will shape how others perceive you. Then relax and enjoy the conversation.

Your focused attention is one of the critical variables in the success of any meeting because *the level of listening and attention in the room shapes the quality of the speaking*. If the group is attentive, it becomes easier for those speaking to be authentic—to say exactly what they are thinking and feeling. People then feel better about themselves and what they have contributed. To be self-expressed and to be heard are important aspects of feeling part of a group. This happens easily in a small group of four or five because the physical proximity naturally creates attention. In large groups, participants must focus on being attentive in order to create the same effect.

Go into every meeting prepared to *devote yourself to each person in the conversation*. This level of attention will always add value to your meetings—in fact, to all of your conversations. As you focus on listening in meetings, you will notice that most people end up speaking directly to you, making eye contact with you, because they naturally move their focus to the person paying attention to them. In a world of multitasking and technology, you might be the only person in the room truly listening.

Commit yourself to the meeting—no distractions

"Multitasking arises out of distraction itself."

—Marilyn vos Savant, American writer

Distractions are harmful to meetings—and multitasking is a distraction both to the person doing it and to the other people in the group. "The research is almost unanimous, which is very rare in social science, and it says that people who chronically multitask show an enormous range of deficits," explains Clifford Nass, coauthor of a Stanford study on multitasking. "They're basically terrible at all sorts of cognitive tasks—including multitasking."

Multitasking has no place in meetings. You may think you are able to follow a conversation as you do something else. But your mind does not actually hear and think two things at the same time. It simply switches back and forth very fast. The moment you look at your smartphone and read that text, you miss what is said in the meeting.

The harm in multitasking is twofold. First, your attention matters to everyone else in the room—especially to the person speaking. Speaking to a group that is not paying attention is distracting at the least and hurtful at worst. People identify with their own speaking, so if you aren't paying attention to what they say, you send the message that you're not paying attention to them as a person.

Second, if you're multitasking, you miss the subtleties in what people say and the nonverbal cues in how they say it. If you are distracted, you miss what is not said. You miss being able to build on their thinking. You may be able to keep up with the gist of their words, but you will likely miss most of what they are actually saying.

7

PARTICIPATE

I know I'm fighting uphill here. Recently a colleague was discussing guidelines for a group's virtual meetings. Someone suggested that everyone agree not to work on their computers during the conference call. One supervisor objected because he thought it would interfere with the productivity of some of his people who were exceptional at multitasking!

Another study showed that only about 2 percent of people are any good at multitasking. "People can't multitask very well, and when people say they can, they're deluding themselves," argued MIT neuroscientist Earl Miller in a National Public Radio interview. "The brain is very good at deluding itself."

So don't delude yourself. Be fully present in every meeting—fully focused on the conversation at hand.

The second component: Be patient

A saying that has served me well when waiting in life—in airports, in traffic—is *There is no place to get to*. It's also a perfect companion to being attentive. When you are listening, set aside your impulse to jump into the conversation. Wait for the other person to finish. There will be plenty of time to ask a question or make a comment when the other person is finished. Slow down and stop anticipating when you might get a chance to speak.

Here's the hard part: Don't step in when there's a pause. Wait and see if he or she has something more to add. My friend Larry tells the story of going home and asking his son, Ellis, to tell him about his day. Ellis replied, "Only if you promise not to steal my pauses."

You may have read some of Judy Brown's wonderful work on dialogue, where she cites the example of providing a prop to slow people down. The rule is you can only speak when you have the talking stick or marker, and you can keep it until you have finished. It's a dramatic way to get people not only to stop interrupting, but also to wait to see if the other person will start talking again.

The third component: Be nonjudgmental

"In true dialogue, people learn to listen to one another, to hear each other's ideas without judgment—and learn a new way of being together. This is part of what I consider dialogue—for people to realize what is on each other's minds without coming to any conclusions or judgments."

—David Bohm, American theoretical physicist

Being nonjudgmental is a tough one because the human mind is wired to continually assess and make judgments. The mind is fast— very fast. Think about your ability to drive ten miles home and, when you get there, you realize you don't remember making any of the turns or stops along the way. On familiar roads, you assess and judge automatically, actually quite safely.

On the other hand, American psychologist Carl Rogers, in his book *On Becoming a Person*, noted how this capacity to assess and judge can interfere with true communication:

> *The major barrier to interpersonal communication lies in the very natural tendency to judge—to approve or disapprove of the statements of the other person. . . . Our first reaction to most of the statements which we hear from people is an immediate evaluation, or judgment, rather than an understanding of it. When someone expresses some feeling or attitude or belief, our tendency is, almost immediately, to feel "that's right," or "that's stupid," "that's reasonable," "that's incorrect." Very rarely do we permit ourselves to understand precisely what the meaning of the statement is to him.*

7

PARTICIPATE

Given the hardwired nature of this tendency to assess and judge, it isn't productive to try to stop doing it. Still, because it can get in the way of your ability to understand and support others, there are ways to keep this judgmental mechanism at bay: Remind yourself that the other person's views are as legitimate as yours. Be curious. Give the person speaking the benefit of the doubt; assume positive intent. When negative thoughts do occur, notice them and then set them aside and intentionally refocus on listening for clarity, understanding, and value.

The fourth component: Listen for something specific in each conversation

One powerful way to get more out of conversations and reduce your tendency to be judgmental is to choose to listen for something in particular. If you do, you will notice things you might otherwise miss.

Usually we listen to follow and understand what is being said. Listening with something in mind allows you to hear new information and have more insights about the people involved in the conversation. The "TRY THIS" box below gives you four candidates to explore.

TRY THIS

☐ Listen for what others are interested in or care about.

☐ Listen for the value being created in the conversation.

☐ Listen for what each person is dealing with in his or her area.

☐ Listen for what you appreciate about each person.

PAUL AXTELL   PARTICIPATE TO HAVE IMPACT   175

Practice focused speaking

*"Focus in speaking has to do with saying what you mean
in a way that can be understood, respected,
and considered relevant."*

—Tim Gallwey, *The Inner Game of Work*

In meetings, your speaking must be more focused than when you are at a party or sitting around a campfire. Focused speaking will do more for cutting down time spent in meetings than anything else—except, perhaps, keeping the conversations on track.

Focused speaking has four components: it is clear, concise, relevant, and respectful.

The first component: Be clear

Being clear requires precise language. People often use general terms without ensuring that everyone has the same understanding of them. General language is useful because it shortens conversations, but only as long as everyone understands what is being said. Being specific adds clarity. For example, it's easy to compliment someone on doing a good job, but it's far more impactful to list three specific things you liked about what they did. Or you might share your concern that employees feel as if no one cares about them, but you add clarity when you express what exactly they are saying, doing, or not doing that gives you that impression.

The surest way to achieve clarity is to give people permission to ask questions if they're unclear. As a participant, give yourself permission to ask.

7

PARTICIPATE

The second component: Be concise

Being concise means getting to the point quickly. There are two immediate ways to work on this:

- **Set up your speaking.** Saying "I have two points to make" not only tells people what is coming, it helps you organize your speaking.

- **Provide only enough explanation to achieve clarity.** Add extra detail or examples only if someone asks for them. Make your point and then look at your audience to see if anyone needs clarification. Adding unnecessary examples wastes time. Adding explanation that isn't asked for can be interpreted as being defensive.

An exception: Sometimes you may want to say something in a meeting without the constraint of being concise. You may not be sure exactly what your point is or how best to say it. That's fine. Just set up your speaking with the group before you start:

> *"With your permission, I'd like to think out loud for a minute or two."*

Don't wear out your welcome

It's difficult to speak effectively if you speak all the time. If you are interested in leadership, consider this: One of the leadership characteristics looked for is quality of thinking, and the quality of your thinking is in part revealed by your speaking. Speaking less is usually more powerful than speaking more. No matter how brilliant you are, if you speak longer or more often than you should, people will lose respect for you.

To speak effectively, you can't speak all the time. You want people to know that when you speak, you intend to add value. You aren't speaking just to be speaking. Being concise helps you stand out as someone who is disciplined, prepared, and professional.

May I take the scenic route?

One of my clients and friends was a brilliant project manager. Bob also loved motorcycles and long camping trips with friends. His speaking style was descriptive and full of examples and side excursions—to a fault: a great style for around the campfire, but an inefficient and maddening style in business meetings. Fortunately, Bob was also amazingly willing to be coached and accept confronting feedback. We worked to eliminate the excessive detail—examples and explanations that weren't necessary to make his point. The last few years we worked together, he often started with, "How much time do you have, Paul? Want the direct route or the scenic route?"

Is it OK if I don't speak?

Not everyone has to speak in every meeting or as often as others. You want to be thoughtful and responsible for how you contribute to the conversation. Still, if you don't usually speak up in meetings, you owe it to yourself—and the group—to consider these questions:

- *Do I have ideas I am not contributing?*
- *Do I have insights or thoughts about improving the group process that would be useful if expressed?*
- *Are there times when I am not aligned with where the group ends up in a conversation, yet I am not expressing my perspective?*
- *Do others in the group have a sense that I'm actively participating?*

If you are naturally quiet, think about the topic ahead of time and speak early. Or you might help summarize the conversation. Be willing to say what needs to be said. Set a high bar for yourself.

7

PARTICIPATE

TRY THIS

☐ Listen for opportunities to contribute to the conversation.

☐ Notice when you have an idea to share but don't speak.

Confronting my comfort zone

I know how hard it is to speak up in meetings. In part it's because I was one of those quiet, soft-spoken people. I was an engineer who began working in a factory right out of college, and it took my supervisor, Kurt Frank, to shake me out of my reticence. I'd been on the job about five weeks when Kurt came into my office on a Friday afternoon. Here's what he said to me:

> Paul, I've been in quite a few meetings with you since you began this job. In most of the meetings, you are the lead engineer. You haven't spoken yet, and I'm here to tell you it's unacceptable. So beginning Monday, you are on probation, and you will speak at least twice in every meeting or at the end of that day, I will fire you. Have a nice weekend.

Now, I knew that not speaking in life didn't work. But Kurt was the first person who cared enough and considered it part of his job to make me understand that and move out of my comfort zone. I got the message: If you don't speak in meetings, you don't add value. You might as well not be there.

The rest of the story: Kurt came in on Monday and told me it was true, and he was going to call on me at times to help me out. He also set me up to teach a problem-solving and decision-making course once a month to develop my speaking skills. Here we are, forty years later, discussing meetings—thanks to Kurt.

The third component: Be relevant

Being relevant means your remarks add value to the topic being discussed. Before you speak, ask yourself these questions:

- *Will what I want to say add value and move the conversation ahead?*
- *Am I making a point or providing content that relates directly to the issue at hand?*

Then after you speak in a meeting, take the time to reflect on your speaking. Were you clear, concise, relevant, and respectful? Use the chart on page 182 and give yourself a simple rating of 1 to 5, taking note of what you spoke about and what you might do differently next time.

You can also ask a colleague to observe your speaking and keep score for you. With this awareness tool, you will begin to correct yourself.

If what you have to say doesn't add value, don't say it

Often the best thing to say is nothing. Effective people aren't compelled to jump in; they don't speak unless what they have to say moves the conversation forward. Even brilliant ideas are sometimes best left unsaid when not relevant to the current discussion.

There are also times when you should let the group conversation speak for you. If your ideas and concerns have already been expressed, don't add them again. Learn to recognize when, even though you have something more to say, it just doesn't add anything to say it.

The fourth component: Be respectful

In addition to being clear, concise, and relevant, you want to speak with respect. Respectful speaking lets people know there is room for them to see it differently. It means using a tone of voice that communicates your intention to add value to the conversation without expecting it to go your way. It means using language that is civil, courteous, and easy to listen to.

We all have different speaking styles, and part of being remarkable in a group setting is being aware of the strengths and weaknesses in your own style. This is not about changing who you are in any fundamental way. It is about developing the ability to improve your speaking style over time to be more effective.

7

PARTICIPATE

Humor can backfire

I admire and enjoy being with groups who have fun together. Be careful about humor, however.

Johnny Carson, on *The Tonight Show*, often made fun of himself. It was called self-deprecating humor. But the tone of humor has changed since then.

"The nature of our humor in this country has evolved or devolved in the last fifty, sixty years depending on your point of view," says film director Michael Stevens. "Put-down humor is the source of all humor these days. It finds an easy target and it goes after low-hanging fruit."

The test for me is this: Did what was said in any way discount the person who just spoke or detract from the last thing that was said? If it detracts in any way, it doesn't work.

But what if I disagree?

> *"We are very likely to have disagreements.*
> *We do not have to be disagreeable."*
>
> —John Wooden, American basketball coach

Do not express disagreement with someone unless it is necessary. If it's about a point that is not central to the conversation, let it pass. If your disagreeing is going to embarrass someone, think twice. If you are hooked emotionally, delay your response. Whatever you resist has a tendency to persist; left alone, it will often disappear.

If you must disagree, do it in a way that shows respect. Start your speaking by taking care of the other person: Make sure you understand the other point of view first and let him or her know you do. Remind yourself that this person's view is valid, given his or her reality—if you had the same background and experiences, you might share the same view. Look for the value in his or her view and communicate it. Then you can express that you see it differently and ask for permission to explain. When you express your concerns, be supportive by acknowledging the other idea, then adding your concern not as a way of resisting, but as an expression of something you feel also needs to be considered.

> *"Josh, I see the value in what you are proposing. If we go with your suggestion, do you have thoughts about how we get the faculty to be supportive?"*

> *"I see what you're saying, and I see it differently. May I explain my viewpoint?"*

Learn to hear and appreciate opposing views as a path to learning. While your first impulse might be to disagree with other people's ideas or comments, there are alternatives. You might ask them to continue speaking about the idea so you more fully understand it. You might simply withhold your contrasting view and see where the conversation goes. You might consider your disagreement as an opportunity to look at the issue from a new perspective—from the perspective of the person speaking. You might view this as an opening for a deeper appreciation of the other person's reality. The trick is not to jump in automatically without consideration for where your disagreement might lead.

Listening and not speaking does not mean that you agree. When the meeting topic is finally concluded, if you are worried that your silence might be interpreted as agreement, make the point at that time.

7

PARTICIPATE

TRY THIS: Rate your speaking

Spoke about:	Clear	1 2 3 4 5
	Concise	1 2 3 4 5
	Relevant	1 2 3 4 5
	Respectful	1 2 3 4 5
Spoke about:	Clear	1 2 3 4 5
	Concise	1 2 3 4 5
	Relevant	1 2 3 4 5
	Respectful	1 2 3 4 5
Spoke about:	Clear	1 2 3 4 5
	Concise	1 2 3 4 5
	Relevant	1 2 3 4 5
	Respectful	1 2 3 4 5

Participate in ways that add impact

We all want to make a difference in life. In meetings, this has tradition-ally meant contributing ideas or agreeing to take on work, but there are a variety of ways to enhance both the conversations that make up a meeting and how others in attendance experience the meeting.

Support the person leading the meeting

While I was waiting to speak at a student leadership program at a uni-versity, eight of the students came up and introduced themselves before the event. They also expressed how much they were looking forward to the session. I was struck by this because, in a typical year of teaching in the corporate world, maybe four or five people will speak with me before the class starts. That's four or five out of a thousand or more!

I acknowledged the faculty member responsible for the program for what he was teaching his students. Jonathan replied, "I wish

I could take credit for it. Those are just the kids who have been involved in 4-H programs!"

The point is that it makes a significant difference to me—and to anyone leading a meeting—if people show support before it starts. You can do this in your organization by asking the person leading the meeting if there is any way you might provide support. Here are some tasks for which your help might be appreciated:

- Welcoming people and taking care of guests

- Setting up coffee or water

- Seeing that the room is set up properly

- Stepping in when the leader needs anything—charts posted, handouts distributed

- Taking notes and writing the meeting summary if that role isn't already assigned

- Offering to observe and provide feedback on the meeting if you know the leader is working on being more skilled at leading effective meetings

Look out for other participants

"Bobby Jones, the legendary golfer, had this sixth sense of noting who in the room was feeling left out and then inviting them into the conversation."

—1998 Masters TV Commentator

It's the responsibility of the person managing the conversation to make sure everyone has a good experience—to take care of them. But it's also a great way to contribute as a participant. What if you were to look for ways to improve someone else's experience of the meeting?

This is a wonderful perspective to take into every meeting. It's not that people need you to look out for them—it's that doing so allows them to be more comfortable and to be at their best. As discussed in the strategy on building relationships, several practices can help improve people's experience of being in a group. Consider these:

Before the meeting begins:

- Greet people individually.
- Check in with people. Ask about their projects, family, weekends.

During the meeting:

- Notice those who are trying to speak and invite them into the conversation.
- Use people's names, especially when their comments influence your thinking.
- Listen and pay attention when each person speaks—make eye contact and avoid distracting behavior, such as checking your smartphone.
- If people are interrupted, ask them to finish their thoughts if the leader doesn't do so.
- If you feel the group conversation skipped over what was said or asked, invite people to restate their point or question.
- Check back with people if you think they might have something else to add.
- Take note if you find yourself thinking about someone not in attendance but who would appreciate being told about what was covered.

After the meeting:

- Thank people whose contributions added value.
- Take time to say good-bye.

Avoid nine common mistakes:

1. Speaking more often or longer than necessary.
2. Providing more detail or examples than people need.
3. Using humor that discounts the previous speaker or the conversation.
4. Using nonverbal behavior that is distracting or suggests inattention.
5. Being blunt to the point where people see it as uncivil.
6. Not being willing to take on work between meetings.
7. Resisting someone else's comments rather than working to understand them.
8. Not speaking up when the conversation is off track or unclear.
9. Not treating the meeting as if it really matters.

Ask for what you need to participate fully

You might not feel comfortable commenting on how the meeting is going, but you do have the right to ask for whatever you need to be effective. If you need clarity, ask for it. If you need a chance to be heard, ask for it. Whatever you need, ask for it. Chances are someone else in the group will appreciate your asking.

> "Before we start, I would like permission to use my laptop to take notes."

> "I think this topic is critical, and I request that we devote enough time to it so every person in the room can share their thinking."

Be clear on outcomes and process

Always check to see if you are clear about what outcomes are expected from the conversation and how you can contribute to getting there. If you aren't clear, it's likely others are not. Asking at the beginning is easier than once the conversation has started. Helping the group set up a conversation properly is a powerful way of adding value to the meeting.

> *"Before we get into this topic, could you explain where you want to be at the end of the discussion?"*

> *"Sarah, is there something specific that you are looking for from us?"*

Usually you can rely on the person leading the meeting to make sure each topic discussion is productive and inclusive. As a participant, you can also influence how conversations are conducted by keeping your eye on process.

Help keep the conversation on track. When you embrace the value of keeping a conversation on track to reach the stated objectives, you will begin to notice several things. You will notice more quickly when a conversation changes to something not directly related to this topic. You will develop a sense of whether the group is making progress. And with your eye on the end point, you will begin to see what the next logical step in working on the topic might be.

> *"It would be helpful if someone could summarize the conversation for me at this point."*

> *"It seems to me that we've moved away from our original plan for this topic. I want to call this to the attention of the group and see if we want to hold the current conversation for another time."*

Notice what's missing and provide it. In addition to looking at meetings in terms of what works and what doesn't work, it's helpful to look for what is missing that you might provide. What would make the meeting work better if it were present?

> *"I'm struggling to make sense of our conversation and wonder if we might stop for a couple of minutes and list on a chart the ideas and concerns we have generated so far."*

"I would appreciate hearing from some folks who will be impacted by this decision."

Commit to specific actions. Part of being an effective group member is being willing to take on work. Most people wait until they are asked. Be seen as someone who readily takes on work and then delivers. Don't take on everything, but be an almost automatic yes, instead of an automatic no. Getting work done ultimately determines the success of both meeting and group.

"I like what we've produced in this conversation, and I want to be sure I have correctly noted what you want me to do and by when."

"Do or do not. There is no try."

—Yoda, *The Empire Strikes Back*

One participant takes initiative

After leading a seminar on meetings for a management group in Oregon, I received this note from one of the participants:

Since the seminar, I participated in a meeting with twelve people in which the discussion kept getting sidetracked and derailed while we were attempting to solve a problem. During a scheduled break, I took the time to write the current issues and the strategies to solve each on the whiteboard, so when the team came back, we could have a structured dialogue on which strategy we were going to move forward with to address each problem. The team was able to stay focused and reach a consensus in a short amount of time. I was only a participant in the meeting, but I realized someone needed to take the initiative.

The second issue I have been trying to address is my fatal flaw of interrupting individuals. I guess I can say I have a greater awareness of when others perform the same behavior, but I am still working on the issue for myself.   —Regards, Keith

Practice self-awareness

While it's difficult to watch yourself as you perform, it is possible to become more self-aware, particularly aware of how you interact in meetings. You can reflect on your speaking right after you finish. You can be aware of how fully you listen and pay attention. You can be aware of your posture and nonverbal cues. With reflection over time, the way you interact in meetings will improve.

When working with groups, I often begin by asking folks to acknowledge their colleagues by answering these two questions:

- *Who do you rely on for what?*
- *What do you appreciate about how someone interacts in the group?*

It's a fun, positive conversation that also reminds everyone of what it takes for a group to work together in an effective way. In their responses, the group members honor as well as learn something about each other.

I also ask a few other people to share how they might answer these two questions.

- *What two things do you do in meetings that probably don't work for others in the group?*
- *What don't you do that people would love it if you did?*

It's another light conversation that can reveal common unproductive behavior. Reflect on these questions and identify what these things are for you. Then if you keep them in mind in your meetings, you'll begin to self-correct and contribute at the level you are fully capable of.

The point of these exercises is that self-reflection is a way to improve performance. Work with the questions in the "Try This" box below. Doing so will help you notice things you might not be noticing now. And with every new piece you notice, you give yourself different ways of interacting in a meeting.

You might also ask someone to observe you and give you feedback. You will find much more on feedback in the chapter, "The Art of Learning to Be Effective."

TRY THIS

☐ After each meeting for the next two weeks, reflect on what you said, how you said it, and what impact your comments had on the group conversation.

☐ Reflect on what you bring to a particular meeting or group:

- *What do people rely on you for?*
- *What do they appreciate about their interactions with you?*

☐ Begin to observe people who speak in a way you admire. What is it about what they say or how they say it that elicits respect?

7

PARTICIPATE

"Ask your questions, because then you may elicit answers that someone else desperately needs. Discuss your doubts, because in doing so you may allow others to share theirs."

—Jaida n'ha Sandra, *Salons: The Joy of Conversation*

“Build for your team
a feeling of oneness,
of dependence on one
another and of strength to
be derived by unity.”

—Vince Lombardi
American football coach

Build
Remarkable
Groups

Core ideas:

- How we work together matters.
- Discover the possibility of remarkable groups.
- Create a compelling reason for working together.
- Get to know each other so trust is not an issue.
- Develop guidelines for working together.
- Be responsible for everyone's success.
- Deal with the world in a way others can respect and appreciate.
- Make every meeting count, and be productive between meetings.

"To me, teamwork is a lot like being part of a family. It comes with obligations, entanglements, headaches, and quarrels. But the rewards are worth the cost. With a combination of practice and belief, the most ordinary team is capable of extraordinary things."

—Pat Summitt
University of Tennessee basketball coach

How we work together matters

When groups can work together in a way that's beyond ordinary, they can dream bigger and accomplish far more than individuals working alone. This is the power that can be added to the organization and its goals and projects if you can get your teams to be remarkable.

Some organizations have lost the wisdom and leverage that teams can provide. Many employees complain of being on too many teams or on teams that are not functioning well. Yet organizations must have task forces, project teams, and leadership teams to produce results, develop products, and coordinate programs that simply wouldn't be achieved without a concerted group effort.

The keys to creating teams that match this high expectation lie in getting to know each other, being productive when you meet, and having each other's back when you are apart. Though I don't know you or your group or your organization, my years of experience working with other groups and other organizations have shown that the ideas you will find here have worked, and they worked powerfully.

Reflect on the best experience you've ever had in a group within an organization. What made it special? Your high regard for everyone in the group? The consistent high-quality conversations every time you met? The decisiveness and boldness of the group? The long string of accomplishments you produced together? Probably all of these.

Because we've seen so many examples of ineffective groups, it's easy to forget how special it is to be part of a group that does great work. Improving your meetings is an important first step toward getting your group to be remarkable. People love to be a part of successful teams. In the world of organizations, this means groups that consistently outperform expectations—and where individuals are valued for their contributions and feel as if they are really a part of that collective success.

In the process of improving your meetings, you will become more cohesive—a greater sense of unity is a natural by-product of thoughtfully designed and well-run meetings. This strategy is about working cohesively and effectively in ways that allow a degree of group performance otherwise unavailable.

Discover the possibility of remarkable groups

What does being a remarkable group make possible?

Once you build a remarkable group, good things begin to happen—some you can anticipate and others you cannot. Remarkable groups become:

- **More productive.** Remarkable groups produce results that unaligned individual efforts cannot. Teams working productively together can simply dream bigger and get more done.

- **Resilient.** Remarkable groups can handle bad times and difficult circumstances and come out the other side even stronger. Loss creates resilience, if you can get past it—and remarkable groups can.

- **Able to develop and attract talent.** There probably is no better way to develop talent in individuals than to have them be part of a group that knows how to work together. As the group's reputation grows, you will find it easier to attract talent.

- **Catalysts for change.** If you have one remarkable team, other parts of the organization will notice and rekindle the belief that this level of performance is available to them, too. It's like dropping a pebble in a quiet pond and watching the ripple spread.

Imagine what might become possible for your organization if you build teams that set new standards for accomplishment.

When I work in training programs on building teams or creating remarkable groups, I first start by asking people to answer this set of questions:

- *What does being a remarkable group make possible?*
- *What does it mean to be a remarkable group?*
- *What does it mean to be effective in a group?*

I ask people to come up with seven answers for each question. The intent is to discover the possibilities and practices associated with teams. These three questions also get people on the same page because everyone quickly agrees on the essence of what each question represents.

Next, I share a simple model about being effective as a group.

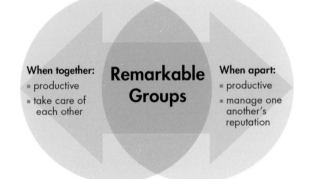

There are two important points here: Groups must be productive during and between meetings, and they must take care of and look out for each other both during and between meetings. You will find this model reflected in the ideas throughout this chapter.

What does it mean to be a remarkable group?

Here's how a Fortune 100 company's leadership team for South America answered the question:

A remarkable team or group is one that:

- *commits to and produces results beyond what is expected,*
- *is not stopped by circumstances or setbacks,*
- *enjoys being together and has productive meetings,*
- *is always aligned and focused on the right things,*
- *can talk about anything in a way that is respectful,*
- *is committed to each member's success, and*
- *welcomes new members and isn't deterred when talent leaves.*

Here are some additional ideas expressed by a group of unit leaders at a major U.S. university:

A remarkable group is one that:

- *respects the individual,*
- *has personal energies focused on common good,*
- *manages its reputation,*
- *is clear about decision processes,*
- *has conversations about what doesn't work,*
- *is responsible for its effect on the world in which it operates, and*
- *calls something a mistake only if the group hasn't learned from it.*

If you create a list for your team, it is likely to be similar. The point is that most people want the same thing, which gives you some common ground on which you can build.

What does it mean to be effective in a group?

One question to ask and resolve for yourself is, *Am I really committed to this group and willing to focus all of my effort to make it successful?* If yes, then the next question is, *How can I help make it happen?*

Start by exploring with each other what it means to be effective in the group setting. This will produce shared expressions for what it means to be a contributing, respected member of a team. In general, if you're effective in a group, it means you're someone who:

- readily takes on work and completes that work reliably,
- is always self-expressed—willing to say what you are thinking,
- treats everyone with trust and respect,
- is willing to compromise for the good of the team,
- is enjoyable to be around and easy to talk to, and
- is not constrained by job titles or roles—does whatever is needed.

> *"One day, I decided to help wherever I could,*
> *& it was almost like magic because I was exactly*
> *what the world needed everywhere I went."*
> —Brian Andreas, Storypeople.com

Create a compelling reason for working together

Many years ago, I did a four-day training program for six teams in a manufacturing company. Each team consisted of six to twelve people. We worked through a series of conversations over the four days, setting up each conversation in the large group, then letting smaller groups work in their natural teams.

8
REMARKABLE GROUPS

The range in their reasons for being teams was widespread. One group simply worked on the same shift and had been told they needed to go to a team-building class. Another had been given one year to turn around the performance of their product or their unit would be disbanded. As you can imagine, the first group struggled, and the second group couldn't wait to get to work. The first group was focused on choosing a name for their team. The second group was working on redesigning their product and convincing management to fund the new product design.

These two examples frame the wide range of where teams can be with respect to having a compelling reason for working together. Most groups will set higher targets when given the opportunity.

Determine your focus for the year

Remarkable groups identify the goals and milestones along the way to achieving their purpose. Identifying goals that require the group to act in an uncommon way and committing to them individually and collectively provides the structure within which to operate together.

Appendix A includes a conversation design that will help you identify your goals—and instill the belief that they can be achieved. It is a series of questions that has proved effective in setting goals and determining focus for the year. The team develops a list for each question, then selects the final goals from the entire set of lists. Once you have discussed and together answered these key questions, you will have clearly identified the compelling reasons for working together in a concerted, focused way.

REMARKABLE GROUPS   8

Get to know each other so trust is not an issue

"I'm convinced that getting everyone together and playing checkers for four days would make our projects more successful. We just don't know each other very well and can't seem to find the time to get to know each other."

—Dave Hughes, Kodak Manufacturing

The most important element in building a group is getting to know one another in a deeper way than is typical in a work situation. If you have solid relationships in place, you react differently to small things that could lead to a loss of trust and respect—either as misunderstandings or small mistakes. Plus, it's easier to raise these issues early before they become obstacles in working together. ***Trust and respect are fragile when you don't have enough relationship depth*** to handle unexpected difficulties or even just the stress of meeting tight deadlines.

Use the relationship-building exercises in appendix B to create more connection among members of your group. It's a matter of having one thoughtful, interesting conversation after another—not just during, but before and after your meetings as well. Many of these exercises focus on listening to one another; in this way, great team members are not unlike great musicians, according to this wonderfully apt quote from musician and bandleader Dave Holland: "The greatest musicians are also the greatest listeners. While individually creative, they're collectively supportive."

Adding new team members

The most important thing about getting new members on board and up to speed is to be intentional. This means laying out a set of activities and conversations that will create the background and information they need to be successful within the team.

- **Help them get to know everyone.** Relationship is everything and can't be taken for granted. When people get to know each other, all interactions become easier. Set up a schedule for each team member to take the new person to coffee or lunch. Look for opportunities to include the newest members in meetings, travel, and activities. Invite them to share about their family, interests, and background, and share your own stories to help them get to know and be comfortable with you.

- **Help them make an impact early.** One aspect of feeling part of the group is knowing that you add value. It's hard to do this without being accountable for specific assignments. Don't wait to give new members a chance to contribute. Ask for their views in meetings. Make lots of requests of them. Acknowledge their contributions.

- **Communicate team agreements and practices.** People must recognize and adapt to the organizational culture. If the team has specific ways of working, be sure to point these out. Reflect and identify what practices the team utilizes. Share these. If you have any complaints about how the new person works, tell them.

- **Let them know it's OK to ask.** It's essential that new members feel completely comfortable in asking questions about anything. Mentoring new members can be formal or informal, but check in with them regularly to see how things are going and ask if they have any questions.

Develop guidelines for working together

The Whitfield School in St. Louis has just two rules for its students:

- Be nice.
- Do the right thing.

These two rules remind me that the most useful and valuable guidelines for a team are straightforward and common sense—and often likely to be missing. A written set of team practices is important because they truly represent what does not ordinarily exist in organizations. It will take awareness and repetition on the part of the team to keep the practices in place. Plus there will always be new team members who can benefit from knowing "how we do things around here."

On the following pages is a template you might use to tailor your own group practices; it's taken from a high-performing group I've worked with and learned from over the years. This group of about forty unit leaders in a college within a large public university created the document to remind themselves about who they wanted to be and what it looked like when their actions were consistent with that intention.

The template reflects an approach that works in the private sector as well, as Thomas Watson, IBM's CEO, expressed: "How did we create the IBM culture? Well, first we sat down and described what we wanted to be true in the future that wasn't true now. Then we asked ourselves, 'When we have that culture, how will we be acting?' Then we saw that we needed to start acting that way right now."

Practices of the College of Agricultural Sciences, Oregon State University

Practices we embrace	Key points in each practice
Manage our conversations so they are effective	Have one conversation at a time, one person speaking at a time. Have someone manage the conversation. Be clear about the outcomes and the process. Be definitive about closure: *Where are we? What happens next?*
Listen respectfully and generously	Pay attention to what the person is saying. Allow people to finish. If you have any doubt that you understood, always verify your understanding. Acknowledge—and truly consider— different perspectives. Check for completion: Is this person finished? Is there anything else?
Communicate with each other completely	If we aren't aligned, say so. If something doesn't work, say so.
Make and keep commitments with one another	Be specific about what the commitments are. Use X by Y (Who will do what by when?) Call if your commitment is in danger of not being fulfilled.

REMARKABLE GROUPS
8

Practices we embrace	Key points in each practice
Be on each other's side	Manage each other's reputation. Be supportive and helpful.
	Be inclusive; invite people who may have an interest or may want to contribute.
	Look out for the interests of our group and our university.
Acknowledge and appreciate each other	Look for what can be acknowledged; tell people what you appreciate about them and their work.
	Practice acknowledgment frequently.
	Be authentic.
Be aligned on our strategic intent and current projects	If we are not aligned, communicate.
	If progress slows or stops, acknowledge it.
	Keep resources and energies focused.
	Always be looking to stop low-impact programs and activities.
Practice transparency and sharing information	Ask for what you need.
	Anticipate what others in the group might want to know.
	If asked for information, share everything you know.

"Tolerance of different ideas is indispensable to group conversation. A tolerant group allows everyone to say what they think and feel, comfortable in the assurance that they will be respected even in the face of disagreement."

—Jaida n'ha Sandra, *Salons: The Joy of Conversation*

Be responsible for everyone's success

This is a perspective for the group as a whole to adopt. Being responsible for the others' success means you are constantly looking for what you might do to support other members of the group.

It also means doing whatever it takes to have the group be successful rather than putting all of your energy into your own agenda. Start with noticing how people are doing and offering your support when you think it will be useful. Recognize that the group is not successful unless each individual in it is successful. The beauty of this is that, by focusing on each other's success, you end up advancing your own.

Individual work is vital to any organization's success, but in addition to being focused on your own performance, being part of a group requires being just as interested in other people's success. Imagine the power if each member of the group were to bring this attitude to the table.

The poet Rainer Maria Rilke says it more eloquently: "If I don't manage to fly, someone else will. The Spirit wants only that there be flying. As to who happens to do it, She has only a passing interest."

Take care of each other's reputation

"We argue and then we let the conversation settle down before we leave. And when we leave, we've got each other's back!"

—French engineer in an international training program

In your group, do you have each others' backs? When you are a high-performing group, you do. When you have each other's backs, it means you don't say or do anything that will undermine any member of the group. You don't gossip or whine about a group member, even if you are frustrated with them.

Nor do high-performing group members listen to discounting conversations about another team member without speaking up. Members of successful groups realize they must be on each other's side—colleagues who not only look out for each other in accomplishing goals and tasks, but who support each other in the truest sense of the word.

Whether inside or outside the workplace, you can see this "I've got your back" attitude in action: Great parents are on the side of their kids. The best coaches relate well to each and every person on their teams—the all-stars as well as the players on the bench. No matter what happens, they know that to be successful, they need to be there for each other.

Dealing with gossip

Gossip doesn't produce anything worthwhile, yet we all do it. Maybe we do it to belong or to be a part of the conversation or because judging and assessing others in a negative way somehow makes us feel superior.

That's not what happens in remarkable groups. Unless what you have to say about someone is positive, don't say it. If you hear someone complaining about someone else, ask them to speak to the person directly.

It's easy to accept gossip as something we can't change because everyone does it. But if we do that, we lose all hope of truly having a remarkable group or organization.

> *"You are the good guys. You should act like it."*
>
> —Ainsley Hayes, *West Wing* character

Gossip: What options do you have?

What to do:

- Join in. (Not a great choice!)
- Listen, hoping it ends.
- Excuse yourself.
- Change the subject.
- Confront it.

What to say if you choose to confront it:

- *"I don't like this conversation. Let's talk about something else."*
- *"This conversation doesn't work for me. Does it seem worthwhile to you?"*
- *"Sounds like you have an issue with Will. Have you spoken with him about this?"*
- *"Why are you telling me this?"*

Deal with the world in a way others can respect and appreciate

If you are working in a group, it's important to work in a way that leads others to trust and respect you. In his book, *Letters to My Son*, American spirituality author Kent Nerburn states that all relationships exist in a bigger framework, and if you don't respect how your manager or partner or colleagues deal with the larger world, the relationship will erode. The point is to have high standards for how you deal with the world because others will notice if you do not.

These are the characteristics on which to put your focus:

- *Am I reliable? Do I readily take on work and deliver on my commitments?*

- *Do I treat people the same regardless of their position?*

- *Am I loyal to those who are not present?*

- *Do I use language that expresses respect?*

- *Am I discreet and mindful about what someone shares with me?*

- *Am I responsive beyond what is expected?*

- *Do I notice people who are not included?*

- *Do I respect other people's time?*

- *Am I approachable, easy to talk to, and enjoyable to be around?*

- *Do I add value to every meeting and conversation I'm in?*

Conversations not worth having

When my daughter, Amy, was in middle school, she and I held each other accountable for the quality of our conversations. If one of us overheard the other engaging in a conversation in which we didn't see value, we would make a light comment to remind each other of how we wanted to be in the world. For example, I might hear Amy on the phone with a friend making discounting statements about another classmate. If so, I would say, "Amy, that doesn't seem like a conversation worth having." Or if Amy heard me whining about my boss, she would say, "Doesn't seem like a conversation worth having, Dad."

We all slip from time to time and gossip about others who are not present, or we whine about someone's actions, or we blame others for our lack of performance. We need to remind ourselves that we are better than this—we don't want to define ourselves by a pattern of conversations that do not add value.

Make every meeting count, and be productive between meetings

One purpose of meeting is to set up the work you will accomplish *between* meetings. If you are not productive when you meet, it is impossible to maintain an awesome team. If you are not productive between meetings, the group and the project will suffer.

To maintain the momentum you've generated during your meetings, pay attention to these four key variables:

1. **Make specific commitments in time:** Be deliberate when wrapping up each meeting topic, especially when checking for alignment and listing the next steps or actions to be taken. Emphasize the agreement to communicate if a commitment gets in danger of not being completed.

2. **Make notes:** Capture the actions in some form of meeting summary and distribute it on the same day.

3. **Follow through:** Assign someone to track the commitments made, and follow up with people at agreed-upon intervals between meetings.

4. **Be responsible and tolerant:** Be understanding when people cannot deliver what they promised. Be less understanding if they don't let you know in time for you to do something about it.

A final thought: Creating and maintaining a group that is remarkable is hard work on the part of each member and the group as a whole, not just the leader. Extra time, energy, and effort are required for working as a group.

TRY THIS

☐ Notice what you say outside of the meeting about the group or individuals in the group. If it is not positive, learn to keep from saying it.

☐ Look for what you might offer in terms of support to other team members.

☐ Invite the newest member of the team to coffee and ask if he or she would like support.

☐ Think about how you might ask the group to support you.

"When most oarsmen talked about their perfect moments in a boat, they referred not so much to winning a race, as to the feel of the boat, all eight oars in the water together, the synchronization almost perfect. In moments like these, the boat seemed to lift right out of the water. Oarsmen called that the moment of *swing*."

—David Halberstam
The Amateurs

8
REMARKABLE GROUPS

" If you want to learn how to do something, you have to be willing to appear foolish. You have to start doing the thing before you know how—you simply have to start at that place. You'll mess up more often than you get it right at first, if you are really throwing yourself into it. Then, little by little, your practice and bravery at risking looking foolish will give way to increasing levels of mastery, and then you'll have a new skill. "

—George Leonard
American author and educator

The **Art of Learning** to Be Effective

Core ideas:

- Attention and awareness provide access to the level of performance you want to achieve.

- Focus on key variables.

- Practice mindfulness.

- Force time for reflection.

- Debrief experiences with someone else.

- Front-end load to give your mind something to work with.

- Keep a journal of your insights.

- Learn to manage distraction—including multitasking.

- Ask a trusted colleague to observe you and provide candid feedback.

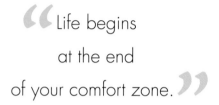

" Life begins
at the end
of your comfort zone. "

—Neale Donald Walsch
American author

Attention and awareness provide access to the level of performance you want to achieve

Each of the ideas about learning in this chapter shaped my journey in training and in life. This chapter has been included both to help you understand the thinking expressed throughout the book and to show you the best way to work with the ideas.

These core ideas about learning apply to every aspect of life. To gain clarity around each of these ideas, you might apply them to an area of life where you are clearly in learning mode. For example, you might consider these ideas in the context of raising children, playing golf, or learning a new skill at work. In this book, we have applied them to meetings.

Get in touch with your incredible ability to learn

Children are amazing when it comes to learning. When they get a new idea, they practice it until they can reproduce it anywhere. Open–closed. Up–down. Soft–hard. They are curious and they love to learn something new. When they are small, children are focused and not easily distracted. They are in the moment. They are keenly aware and have an openness that is exquisite. We need to get back to being as aware and as open and as focused as we were when we were young children.

"Every act of conscious learning requires the willingness to suffer injury to one's self-esteem. That is why young children, before they are aware of their own self-importance, learn so easily."

—Thomas Szasz, Hungarian psychiatrist

TRY THIS

☐ Choose a learning perspective for meetings—go into each one prepared to observe and learn as much as you can about what makes them successful.

☐ When you are around small children, watch them learn and remind yourself what it's like to be open and curious and fine with not knowing all the answers.

Focus on key variables

In every discipline, there are a vital few things to be aware of—to train yourself to notice and pay attention to—that make all the difference in your performance.

During an interview, St. Louis Cardinal baseball pitcher Adam Wainwright discussed how he approached each game. He said he always set goals for himself in terms of innings completed, walks, and total pitches thrown. Then he said he always had a process goal, too, such as throwing strikes on the first pitch to 70 percent of the hitters or throwing 30 percent of his pitches on the inside half of the plate. In other words, Wainwright knows that working on the right process variables adds to his capability.

The same holds true in meetings. If you want to build your capability, begin to practice with the key variables—those elements that have the most impact on success.

LEARNING

Key variables for designing and leading meetings:

- Have permission to manage the conversation.
- Give everyone the freedom to say or ask anything.
- Have clear outcomes defined for each topic.
- Be clear about the process to be followed.
- Have one conversation at a time with one person speaking at a time.
- Ensure everyone else is listening and paying attention.
- Take care of everyone throughout the conversation.
- Take each conversation to completion and next steps.

Key variables for participating in meetings:

- Be clear about outcomes and process steps.
- Ask for what you need to participate effectively.
- Practice focused speaking and be self-expressed.
- Practice focused listening.
- Take care of people; notice who is not yet in the conversation.
- Commit to specific actions.

> **TRY THIS**
>
> ☐ Use each meeting as an opportunity to develop meeting mastery. In every meeting for a series of about ten, pick something to look for from the lists above. Make notes on what you notice. Then pick something else for the next ten meetings, and so on.

LEARNING

The Path to Awareness, Insight, and Choice

"Critical variables can be identified for any situation or activity. A variable is not an instruction to do something. It is a focus for attention."

—Tim Gallwey, *The Inner Game of Work*

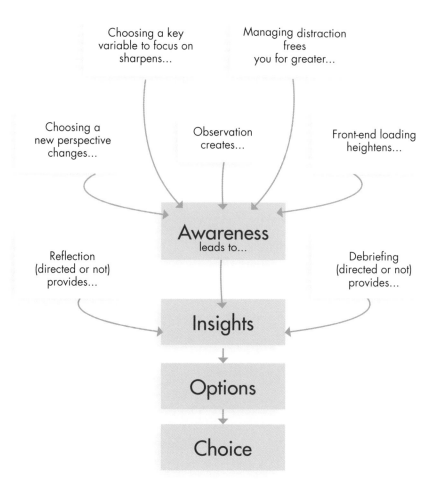

This chart shows all the ways you can increase your level of awareness, which will in turn change how you respond to life.

Practice mindfulness

"The range of what we do is limited by what we fail to notice, and because we fail to notice that we fail to notice, there is little we can do to change until we notice how failing to notice shapes our thoughts and deeds."

—Daniel Jay Goleman, American psychologist

We need to remind ourselves to notice what is there to be seen. As Yogi Berra said, "You can observe a lot just by watching."

We've been raised to think that taking action is the first step in changing our behavior. But that isn't the best route to being more effective—awareness is. I recall working with a gentleman who interrupted people constantly. He realized it didn't work for others, but he just couldn't stop doing it himself. So I asked him to go into every meeting and take notes on the following:

- Who interrupts whom?
- What is the impact on the conversation that was interrupted?
- What is the impact on the person who was interrupted?

What do you suppose happened? Of course, the gentleman stopped his own interrupting. Awareness is the first step and sometimes all it takes to make meaningful change happen.

> **TRY THIS**
> ☐ Notice what there is to notice on your drive to work. This will give you practice with the idea of observing and seeing what there is to see. This is the first step in being mindful.
> ☐ Go into a meeting with the self-instruction to just hear and see what is there to be heard and seen.

LEARNING

Force time for reflection

"Without reflection, we go blindly on our way,
creating more unintended consequences,
and failing to achieve anything useful."

—Margaret J. Wheatley, American author

If you are committed to improving your performance in some area, you probably make time for reflection. For example, if you play golf, you often replay the round stroke by stroke in your mind. If you play poker or bridge competitively, you replay almost every hand as you reflect on your play afterward.

Effective people find time for reflection. It's not easy because of the demands of life and the constant pull of distractions. Still, if you want to learn each day from your experiences, the practice of reflection is critical. Reflecting is different than noticing in the moment. Reflection occurs after an experience or at the end of the day. Effective people try to find time for at least forty-five minutes of reflection per day. Sounds impossible, doesn't it?

Maybe not. When you're in your car alone, don't turn the radio on. Two things might happen: If you have a problem, your mind will go to work on solving it. If you have no current problems, your mind will do something creative. This also applies to those times when you go for a run or hop onto the treadmill. I understand it's easier to get started if you have some great music playing. But once you are into the walk, switch off the music and give your mind a chance to reflect.

Brain scientists say insights last from five minutes to a couple of hours. Given the pace of our lives, I think it's probably closer to five minutes for most of us. Build in some time for reflection, and you'll not only retain more insights, you'll reduce some of the stress in your life.

LEARNING

TRY THIS

☐ Each day find fifteen to twenty minutes to reflect on an important conversation.

☐ Don't put the car radio on while driving or the earbuds in while running or cycling and notice where your mind goes.

☐ After every meeting, take a moment and note what you learned.

Debrief experiences with someone else

"Experiential learning is overrated. Unless you debrief your experience, you miss out on much of the learning."

—Tim Gallwey, *The Inner Game of Tennis*

A new supervisor in a factory shared with me that he had flown spy plane missions for twelve years. When I asked him how much time they spent debriefing the flights, he said it was at least twice if not four times the length of the flight!

Debriefing is similar to reflection except it is an active process done with another person. Usually we only debrief significant events, such as accidents in the factory or the loss of a client account. Some groups have added five minutes at the end of each meeting to talk about what worked and what didn't, but this is assessing and judging—it's not debriefing.

If you send someone to work in China for three weeks, the typical learning assignment is to ask the person to make a twenty-minute presentation to the work group upon return. This is not a very powerful setup for learning. Contrast that approach with this one:

> *"Andrea, on your next trip to China, this is what I want you to do: Spend twenty minutes at the end of each day listing*

ten insights you had that day about yourself, about working in China, about interacting with peers, or any other insights related to the work you were doing that day. Then choose the insight you think is most valuable long term, and send me an e-mail describing it. In addition, I want you to call me at the end of each week and answer these questions for twenty to thirty minutes: What are you noticing? What has become clear to you in the past week?"

That would be debriefing the experience for maximum learning.

Another level of clarity and more insights are available in a conversation between two people. Push yourself to keep asking, *"What else?"* It's a bit like peeling an onion—with layer upon layer of insights. It's also important to have a colleague or family member with whom you can share your insights and observations on a regular basis. Who might you ask to do this with you? Who would love to be included in your learning or have your support with their own development?

TRY THIS

☐ After important meetings, schedule forty-five minutes to debrief with someone, perhaps over lunch or on a walk. Use these questions: *What did you notice during the meeting? What insights do you have? What are you now thinking about? What might you have done differently?*

☐ If any of your employees are working on meeting skills, provide support by debriefing with them once or twice a month over coffee.

LEARNING

Front-end load to give your mind something to work with

Our minds are brilliant at making connections between two different ideas or pieces of data if we give them something to work with and the time to work with it.

When I was small, my great-grandparents lived on a farm in South Dakota. One of my chores was to go out to the pump and bring in water several times a day. To make the pump work, you first had to prime the pump by pouring the water from the coffee can into the pump. One of the mistakes I made once, but only once, was not filling the coffee can after I had filled the water bucket for the house.

Our minds are like pumps—they need something to get started on, something with which to work.

You've heard the saying, "Necessity is the mother of invention." That's part of it—having a desire to create or invent. Then you must have something to work with—ideas from which to create. That's front-end loading. Then you give your mind time to work with these ideas, preferably at its own pace and in its own time. It often helps to do something else while your mind churns. Your mind will even work while you are sleeping or on long walks, runs, or drives where you aren't distracted by anything.

I first heard the term *front-end loading* on National Public Radio. A young songwriter from Canada was being interviewed, and the conversation went something like this:

NPR: How do you come up with a song?

WRITER: Well, I front-end load, and then I wait.

NPR: Can you give us an example?

LEARNING

WRITER: Sure. I wanted to write some songs about Marilyn Monroe. First, I spent a week watching all the movies in which she had a lead role. Then I went to a gallery and spent hours looking at photographs. Then I read a couple of books about her. Then I organized the next week so I didn't have anything really going on—just relaxing and doing nothing—and I just waited for the songs to appear…and they did.

For this artist, pre-work was necessary—ideas did not appear magically as she was just sitting around. As in my youth, she needed to prime the pump.

You've likely had a similar experience when you've gone to bed still thinking about an issue or a problem, then woken up with an insight or clarity about what to do next. Think about doing this in a more deliberate way around the ideas associated with meetings.

TRY THIS

☐ Read a section or chapter of this book for fifteen minutes, twice a week, and then relax and wait for the insights and connections to appear as you attend meetings.

☐ In meetings, split your note-taking paper into two sections. Use the left-hand two-thirds for notes on the topics that are discussed. Use the right-hand third of the page to record your insights about the meeting process.

LEARNING

Keep a journal of your insights

*"A moment's insight is sometimes worth
a life's experience."*

—Oliver Wendell Holmes, American jurist

As noted earlier, neuroscientists say that new insights last between five minutes and a couple of hours. In other words, they disappear unless you have some kind of system for capturing them. A journal serves as a wonderful way to reinforce insights and keep them available for future reference and reflection.

I realize you are busy, but not learning from your experiences doesn't make sense if you are committed to improving. Having insights is not enough. The same scientists insist that the best way to change behavior is to work with an insight repeatedly over time. This is similar to what happens in physical training, where you are a certain number of reps away from having the muscle memory in place for that new yoga pose or golf swing so it will be there reliably, even under stress. This same notion of repetition applies to soft skills such as speaking, listening, and managing conversations. Just add *notice, notice, notice* to *practice, practice, practice*. Reflection and noticing are the equivalent of practice, and from practice comes mastery.

Recently, it occurred to me that journals serve another purpose. Anne Lamott in *Bird by Bird* says it simply: "Writing causes us to notice."

Learning from experience requires observation and reflection. To gain the value we might derive from both unique and everyday experiences requires that we notice. And writing both causes us to notice and helps us not to lose what we have noticed.

LEARNING

Eva Ogens in *Science Scope* says it another way: "Writing is the currency by which people acquire ownership of ideas; ideas owned are ideas remembered, and ideas remembered are ideas learned."

Learning from experience isn't automatic. When life gets hectic and you run out of quiet time for reflection, it's even more likely you will miss out on learning from your experiences. A journal is a deliberate commitment to make time for reflection and thinking. It's a way of enhancing what you learn from experience. A journal is also a resource you can later draw upon to rekindle an idea, add to your thinking, rebuild awareness, or find something to share with others.

Learn to manage distractions— including multitasking

*"The in-box is flashing again, clamoring for my attention.
Loving novelty, I head in its direction; craving depth,
I do so with a tinge of regret."*

—Bill McKibben, Foreword to *Distracted* by Maggie Jackson

While one path to more awareness is choosing the right things on which to focus, another is reducing the amount of interfering distraction in your life. An experienced engineer in a large factory told me that whenever he gets behind on a design, he goes into the empty factory at night so he can get immersed in his thinking—something he can't do in his cubicle during the day.

Finding blocks of uninterrupted time each week is a key step in being more productive. One powerful idea for starting your day is to complete a task that takes sixty to ninety minutes to accomplish

LEARNING

before you plug into the Internet. Imagine what you might accomplish if you could "get away" for two hours each day!

Another important practice in being effective is to return to doing one thing at a time—reducing the amount of multitasking you do.

Certainly you are capable of doing more than one thing at a time. In fact, new technologies make this one of their selling points. And given how busy you are, it doesn't seem possible to get it all done without multitasking at times. No argument here.

This is partly about doing less multitasking, but it's also about recognizing when you are deliberately choosing multitask. In particular, be aware of the times when, to be effective or to enjoy something, your full attention is required. For example, most creativity requires getting lost in the work. Athletes call this being "in the zone" or playing "out of your mind."

If one of the things you are doing does not require your complete attention, fine; if both things do, reconsider. You can walk on a sidewalk and have a wonderful conversation. You probably can't hike on difficult ground and have the same conversation without being at risk.

Meetings are not a place for multitasking. Your attentiveness matters to others, and you get more out of the conversation if you don't distract yourself by checking technology or doing unrelated work.

A participant in class described her usual level of attention perfectly: "I'm sort of present." This admission is empowering—it unlocks the door to being more attentive, aware, and observant. Acknowledging that you are preoccupied with something else opens the door to being present.

LEARNING

"When we talk about multitasking, we are really talking about attention: the art of paying attention, the ability to shift our attention, and, more broadly, to exercise judgment about what objects are worthy of our attention."

—Christine Rosen, *The Myth of Multitasking*

TRY THIS

☐ Don't allow yourself to do other work in a meeting or take anything into the meeting that might distract you.

☐ Keep side conversations to a minimum.

☐ Create three blocks of time each week for uninterrupted work.

☐ Replace the "smart" technology gadget that connects you with (and pulls you into) the world outside the meeting with a small paper notebook to record your insights. Notice the difference in your focus and participation—and the quality of your insights.

Ask a trusted colleague to observe you and provide candid feedback

"Most importantly, if you're going to ask for feedback, be ready to change."

—David Maister, American business writer

How you participate in meetings is an area where feedback is valuable. You cannot see yourself perform, and it's helpful to get a sense of how you come across to others from colleagues who would treat your request thoughtfully.

LEARNING

Here's a standard by which you might judge your own openness to learning, feedback, and coaching. According to the current literature on coaching, someone who is easy to work with, supervise, and coach:

- is willing to disclose what could be interpreted as flaws, weaknesses, or mistakes;

- is able to ask for, consider, and act upon feedback from others;

- has the ability to observe, reflect, and then share his or her thinking;

- is willing to let colleagues and friends know he or she is being coached or is taking lessons;

- shows appreciation for the process of thinking out loud; and

- realizes that being coached or asking for feedback in no way diminishes a person; rather, it offers the best chance for improvement.

While formal feedback tools like 360-degree instruments can be useful, in-the-moment feedback is more immediate and dynamic. Getting feedback right after a meeting helps you tie the feedback to specific comments or behavior you can readily recall. While feedback during the meeting would usually be distracting, right after works.

Before the meeting, invite a colleague to observe you and provide feedback afterward. By making your request ahead of time, your colleague will have more observations because his or her attention has been primed to notice.

There are two types of feedback: open-ended and focused. Both are useful.

Open-ended feedback seeks information on anything the observer notices about how you participate in meetings—any impression or thought, no matter how small. The beauty of this undirected approach is you will uncover things you didn't think to look for, plus it takes

LEARNING

advantage of the unique experience and perspective of the person observing you.

Focused feedback narrows the lens for the observer and gets you more insights and connections in a particular area. For example, you might ask people to observe you in terms of these questions:

- *Is my nonverbal behavior distracting or sending the wrong message?*
- *Do I introduce my comments in a way that indicates people can push back with me if they want to?*
- *Is my speaking clear, concise, and relevant?*
- *Do I come across as supportive of others in the meeting?*
- *Do my questions help create clarity?*

Giving people specific behaviors to look for ensures you will get data on the areas you most want to work on. With a sharpened focus, their observations are likely to be more helpful to you.

It's also easier for people to provide feedback when your request is focused. If you do something that doesn't work for others, you are usually the last person to know. Without a specific request for feedback, people are not likely to tell you.

Looking for feedback is a serious matter. Don't do it unless you are ready to go to work on what you learn. When you do receive feedback, consider it thoughtfully and thoroughly, and go to work on what you discover. Honor the person providing you this feedback; thank them for helping you to become aware of things you did not realize you were doing (or not doing) in meetings.

LEARNING

We're better when we're being watched

I always like to introduce my wife, Cindy, when she sits in on my seminars so people will feel comfortable walking up to her and interacting with her about ideas in the program.

Last year, while walking to class and thinking about how best to introduce her, I had this insight: "I'm better when Cindy is there!" First, it's because her presence will remind me about things we have discussed in the past, such as "speak slowly" and "interact with people as friends" and "there is no place to get to." Second, it's because I don't want to disappoint her. I realized I am more alert and aware when I am being observed.

Bottom line: As with many other skills in life, knowing the right way to lead or participate in meetings is not sufficient to actually change the way you do it. Changing how you act in meetings requires awareness, attention on key variables, looking for and recording observations and insights, and practice. Getting better at meetings—or anything in life—takes work.

And give yourself a break. You won't get to where you want to be overnight. The beauty of working on meetings is that you have opportunities almost daily to put ideas into practice as you learn. Just take it "bird by bird."

TRY THIS

☐ Ask someone to observe as you lead a meeting or when you're presenting during a meeting.

☐ Begin keeping a journal of daily insights.

"It is indispensable to have a habit of observation and reflection."

—Abraham Lincoln

LEARNING

" For a leader, there is no trivial comment. Something you don't remember saying may have had a devastating impact on someone who looked to you for guidance and approval. "

—Susan Scott
Fierce Conversations

Guidelines for
Managers

Core ideas:

- People matter.

- People want to be connected and included.

- People want to be engaged.

- Meetings are opportunities for engagement.

  - Make the most of chance encounters.

  - Rethink leading your own meetings.

  - Master employee Q&A sessions.

- Adopt an empowering perspective about complaints.

" The chief management tool that also makes learning happen is conversation. And nothing is more personal than good conversation. In the end, conversation comes down to speaking and listening and trust. "

—Alan Webber
Editor, *Fast Company Magazine*

People matter

As a manager, keep two things in mind: You are important to the people who work for you. And you must continually demonstrate that people matter to you. Here are two stories that illustrate these points.

Early in my career, I was moved to a small factory in New Jersey to replace Emerson Eldridge, a supervisor who was retiring after being there for forty years. Emerson was respected and loved by the hourly workforce. In fact, he was godfather to twenty-seven of their kids. A couple of weeks after I replaced him, Dave, the factory manager, called me into his office. Standing outside were fifteen hourly workers. I worked my way through the group, somehow sensing that I should not ask them why they were not working. The conversation with Dave is still vivid:

DAVE: Paul, you love baseball, don't you?

ME: Yes.

DAVE: Well, when a team stops playing well, what do they do?

ME: They fire the manager.

DAVE: Right, why?

ME: Because there is only one of them.

DAVE: Exactly. That's your team standing out there, and they just asked me to fire you. You have an hour to convince them to change their mind.

I walked out of Dave's office and told the group what Dave had said, then I asked them what I needed to do to keep my job. John, the unofficial spokesman of the group, said it very simply: "You need to stop walking past us like we don't exist. We are people, and we want to be treated not only like people, but like friends." I got it—connecting with people became a core focus for me from that moment on.

The second story occurred only a few years ago. At the end of a day in class, Glen, a factory mechanic, offered to take me walleye fishing. I told him that Cindy was along and, while I appreciated the offer, I probably needed to spend the evening with her.

Back at the hotel, I told Cindy about the invitation, and her reply reminded me of the earlier lesson I had learned when I was in my twenties: "Paul, you have to go. Think about what it will mean to Glen if he can walk into the machine shop the next day and tell his buddies that he took you fishing. You must go." I went, and the next day several of Glen's coworkers told me how much it meant to Glen.

For a variety of reasons, we often are not mindful when we interact with employees. These stories provide a reminder of two things: as a supervisor or manager, you matter to people more than you might realize, and by being fully present in each and every conversation you have, you demonstrate that they matter to you.

Why? Imagine what it's like not to have a good relationship with your supervisor. There is an old saying: People don't quit their job; they quit their boss. And if they can't physically leave, they check out mentally. It's just too difficult to keep working at your full potential without being able to talk with and respect your supervisor.

Perhaps the easiest and most powerful way to make a difference with the people who work for you is to talk with them in a way that leaves them feeling you are interested in who they are and what they do.

"People will forget what you said, people will forget what you did, but people will never forget how you made them feel."

—Maya Angelou, American author

People want to be connected and included

In addition to having a personal connection to you, people also love being informed about what is going on in the organization. This is far broader than what happens in any particular meeting. The following example simply illustrates how you might respond when asked questions or when looking for opportunities to share with employees.

When you're asked about a meeting, avoid the typical assessments people make about movies or meetings: "It was good," "It was a long day," or something flippant like, "Well, you know how those meetings go." Instead, this is a time to share a couple of points that resonate with you and might resonate with the person asking. This is not a time to make them ask the perfect question to get access to what you know. Rather, think about what they would like to know and tell them.

> *"Thanks for asking. We covered four topics. I appreciated that the group gained clarity around new employee orientation, and we've asked HR to redesign the workshop. We also spent some time thinking through how we can turn around the employee survey data faster and agreed this year we would complete the process in three months. Was there anything in particular you were interested in?"*

This is not about putting a positive spin on things. This is simply stating what happened and expressing what is true for you with respect to what happened. Moving an organization forward is about choosing the right future, being clear about that future, and then helping people focus on making it happen. These opportunities to talk about the future or the organization are not to be missed. People like to know what management is talking about, and they prefer that management be making progress on important issues. It adds to their sense of being included when you share with them.

MANAGERS

People want to be engaged

People are wired to want to contribute. They love to know that their input is not only welcome but seen as adding value to the organization. When people have a chance to provide input or voice concerns to management, they feel included. They feel as if they belong.

Sometimes people have this thought:

> *I had more to offer, but I never really had a chance to do so; nobody asked for my ideas or seemed to listen when I did voice them.*

To keep this from happening in your group, use these two questions: *What do you think?* and *Where are you with this?*

These questions are similar, yet subtly and powerfully different. The first question is asking for input: *What ideas or concerns do you have about this?* It is designed to surface ideas or issues and get people to contribute their thinking.

The second question asks for where they, personally, stand on an issue. Requesting input is a common meeting design. Asking people where they stand is less common. This question is designed to find out whether they are aligned with and supportive of an idea or decision.

When you ask *What do you think?* and *Where are you with this?* in a sincere way, you honor not only a person's thinking, but who they are as well. These are good conversations to have as normal practice in relationships at home.

After observing a group as they discussed a number of issues, I suggested they try the simplest design I know for reaching alignment:

- Introduce topic.
- Ask: *"Where are you with this?"*

MANAGERS

- Listen.
- Ask: *"What else?"*
- Listen.
- Ask someone else in the group: *"Where are you on this issue?"*
- Listen.
- Ask: *"What else?"*
- Close: *"Okay, here's what I am taking away from this conversation…"* (briefly state your takeaways) *Does that make sense?"* Listen for understanding. Clarify briefly if necessary. *"Thank you."*

This design is valuable because you won't know where people really are about a problem or issue until they tell you. When you ask, *"Where are you with this?"* and do so with an intent to listen and get all views on the table, you can find out where everyone is, and then decide how best to move forward.

For this particular group, participation in the next few conversations was much more balanced, and the quality of those exchanges rose dramatically. I encourage you to try this simple design in your own meetings and see what happens.

When invited to speak

If you are among those invited or requested to speak with a question like *"Where are you with this?"* see it as a good-faith invitation and take the opportunity to express yourself and add to the conversation.

As a supervisor, ask more often; as an employee, respond more often. When both sides are engaged, the conversations work out.

MANAGERS

Do you really want to know what I think?

"We need to stop giving advice. We hire people for their thinking. We should provide the 'guardrails' for their decision making and then let them own and run their part of the business. When they get close to the guardrails, then they owe their manager a conversation."

—Paul Garcia, Manufacturing Engineering Manager

In training programs, when we encourage people to speak up more in meetings, the following concerns are often expressed:

My manager doesn't really want to know what I think. She asks for our input, but she doesn't do anything with what we say.

We have these question-and-answer sessions, but there is never enough time for more than a few questions.

If you complain, you'll hear about it. I have personally been told not to ask difficult questions during quarterly meetings.

Here is the perspective for managers to take on these complaints (and this may surprise you): They are expressions of interest. Most people want to be actively engaged with their supervisors and managers. And if people are complaining, it means they haven't given up—they still hope that speaking up will make a difference. Now, in most work settings, we haven't trained people on how to complain in a powerful but respectful way, so look past how it sounds. Assume that people have their hearts in the right place. Questions don't equal resistance or opposition.

A respected senior executive expresses it this way: "Real poverty is having no voice. I don't know where I saw this or heard this. It has been meaningful to me because I run into people who choose not to share their thinking except when asked, and I make a point of drawing those people out."

This is the perspective to adopt: ***People prefer to have a voice.***

Consider what could happen in your organization if every supervisor or manager who holds a meeting adds to the organization's reputation for being truly interested in what people think. There will always be some managers who find it easier not to seek input, but if the majority do this in a meaningful way, you'll create an organizational norm of being inclusive.

Listening to and valuing your employees' ideas doesn't necessarily mean that you will act on them or even agree with them. That's OK; most employees want to be heard and make a difference, but they understand that management has the final say.

> *"And when you believe your voice adds value…well, let's just say, that belief can make a life-changing difference."*
> —Rachel Macy Stafford, *Hands Free Mama*

Meetings are opportunities for engagement

Meetings offer an ideal place for department heads, managers, and unit leaders to demonstrate their commitment to engage and listen to employees. Let's explore three kinds of meetings and the opportunities they offer you as a manager to connect with your team:

- **Chance encounters** on the factory floor, office hallway, in the parking lot, or on campus
- **Regular meetings** that are scheduled daily or weekly
- **Q&A sessions** with employees

Make the most of chance encounters

This is a request I received from a senior manager: "Paul, I love doing the question-and-answer sessions with large groups of employees. But when I am walking through the factory and someone stops me

MANAGERS

to talk, I'm always uncomfortable and later never feel as if I handled the conversation well." Here's how I responded, and it's advice I offer you as well:

> *The brief, informal conversations you have with people are valuable. You and your managers are important to people. Your people want to have a sense of being in relationship and communication with you. This requires conversation, however brief it may be.*
>
> *When you talk to people casually, you add another positive conversation into the culture. If you are interested in connecting and engaging with people throughout the organization, three hours in short, spontaneous conversations would cover a lot of people. Think of it in terms of eight-minute conversations. If you listen flat-out for three or four minutes, then respond thoughtfully to what is said, both of you will leave feeling it was a conversation worth having and time well spent.*
>
> *The most important thing is to stop and really pay attention. If you don't have time to stop and listen, ask them to call and set up a time to talk. If you have three minutes, let them know you have three minutes, then listen until they are finished. Don't interrupt. When they stop talking, ask what they would like from you. Ask if they want you to do something or if this is just something they want you to know. Then give them a straight response. This can include any of the following (keeping in mind that sincerity on your part is key):*
>
>> *"Thanks for letting me know."*
>>
>> *"Please call and set up more time for us to talk about this."*
>>
>> *"Please take this up with your supervisor and let me know how it goes."*
>>
>> *"I appreciate the conversation, and I'm not going to do anything with this. Is that OK with you?"*

"I don't have an answer for you right now. Please e-mail your question so I can give you a thoughtful reply."

"I actually don't see it the way you do, but I appreciate knowing your view." Then if they ask for your view, share it.

Be careful—it is amazing how many commitments people infer from short conversations. Be clear whether you intend to do something or not.

Just listening and appreciating where they are coming from is a contribution to people. Even though people seem to want certainty and answers, what they really need is a chance to be heard and clarity about what has happened or is going to happen.

People won't always thank you for listening or let you know that your conversation with them made a difference. Trust me. It does.

Treat sensitive conversations and confidentiality appropriately

If you stop and engage with employees, people will share things with you. In particular, if you get a reputation for listening in a sincere, caring way, they will confide in you. When they do, treat their confidence with respect. Verbalizing how you intend to treat what they just told you can not only make them feel more comfortable, it will increase their level of trust in you and the organization. These are things you might say:

"I will respect this conversation by not saying anything to anyone."

"I'd like to share this conversation with…. Would that be OK with you?"

"I need to share this. How do you want me to handle it so it works for you?"

Rethink leading your own meetings

During a leadership team meeting, Tim, a client and manager of the group, opened the morning with, "How is everybody doing?" Most in the group smiled and said they were doing great. Then a couple of people shared some specifics about what their groups were accomplishing.

Then George said, "Frankly, I feel like I'm drowning."

Then someone else brought up something about her group, and the conversation moved on as though George hadn't spoken at all. Neither Tim nor anyone in the group gave any indication they heard the comment, and they certainly didn't acknowledge or respond to it.

Tim didn't skip over George's comment because he didn't care. When he and I discussed this during a break, he said he missed it completely because he was preoccupied with deciding how to introduce the first topic on the agenda. He missed the opportunity to say, "George, thanks for sharing that. I'd appreciate if you would take a couple of minutes and give us all a sense of what you are dealing with."

At a minimum, the comment must be acknowledged and an invitation made to follow up:

"George, I appreciate your honesty. Let's find time to talk at lunch."

The point is, if we slow down and pay attention, people will provide hints or invitations to begin new conversations with them. If you are distracted or rushed, you can miss them altogether.

Contrast this with what Aaron, a senior manager in a Fortune 100 company, says about not leading his own meetings:

Not leading your own meetings can be a wise decision. First of all, I enjoy relaxing and just listening. I don't miss as much when I let someone else lead the meeting. As a manager, having the ability to participate in the discussions with the rest of the team as an equal participant helps create more alignment to key decisions within the team.

By delegating someone to lead my meetings, I'm not seen as driving the agenda or forcing team members to fall in line. It fosters a more collaborative and engaged environment. It also supports more open discussions and debate so that everyone feels their voice is being heard.

From a development standpoint, appointing a leader gives newer team members a chance to demonstrate their leadership qualities. It also provides me with the opportunity to sit "outside" of the discussion and observe the broader team dynamics, assess individual team member contributions, and allow for the team to develop an aligned solution to a problem.

I love the value Aaron sees in asking someone else to lead his meetings. There are two other reasons you might consider doing the same: if you don't have the time to do the necessary design and preparation, or if leading meetings is simply not one of your strengths.

This idea became crystal clear to me when I observed that my client Stan—a brilliant man and a great person—was terrible at running meetings. First, Stan was extremely busy and rarely had time to prepare for meetings—he was often looking at the agenda for the first time as he walked into the meeting. Second, his speaking style was thoughtful, slow, detailed, and meandering. He just enjoyed stepping out of his hectic pace and relaxing in conversation with his group.

Stan was aware that his meetings were not productive, and at times he apologized for his lack of preparation or the lack of progress. Still, it never occurred to him to turn leading them over to someone else. Once it was suggested, he thought it a wonderful idea. The meetings immediately became excellent when one of his aides took over leading them.

MANAGERS

If you choose to have someone lead your meetings...

You may prefer to stay out of a conversation in the beginning so your views do not influence the discussion. That's fine. Still, there will be times when the group wants to know where you stand. Give people permission to check in with you. Let them know they can ask about your views at any time. Not speaking can leave people wondering where you are on an issue or in the overall conversation.

You have a wide range of options when you're asked about your views:

"I'm thinking out loud here and am not set on anything yet."

"Here is my thinking at this point..."

"I don't have strong views on this issue."

"I feel strongly that we need to do something, but I don't know what that is yet."

"I've pretty much decided what I want to do, but I'd like to hear where you are first."

Bottom line: You don't have to facilitate the conversation, but you must play your role by listening, assimilating, providing context, and confirming commitments.

My point is, the ability to run meetings is a core competency. Someone in your group needs to be good at it. Organizations need effective meetings—it matters less who leads them. Even if you do have time to prepare for your meetings and your conversational style is excellent, think about who might be the best person to run the meeting. Who in your group might wish to and be ready to run future meetings for you?

MANAGERS

I'd like you to consider allowing others the opportunity to lead your meetings for several reasons:

- You can only truly focus on one thing at a time. The person managing the conversation is fully occupied keeping the conversation on track, producing the meeting outcomes, and balancing participation levels. It is difficult to facilitate a conversation while devoting yourself to each person who speaks and reflecting upon what is happening in the conversation.

- As supervisor or manager of the group, your attention is best focused on listening and understanding everything that is said. If you have to focus on managing the conversation, your attention is diverted from listening in a profound way.

- You have the default power position already, so if you lead the conversation, you are in essence doubling up on power and control. It's just too tempting for people to go along with whatever you say when you are facilitating the discussion.

- Your attention to each and every person in the group matters, especially when they are speaking about something they feel passionate or upset about.

- You have an organizational perspective that others don't have. If you are participating rather than leading, you'll have a better sense of when adding this perspective would be useful.

- When you add your thinking to the wrap-up for each topic, it gives you the opportunity to capture the value from the discussion and influence what happens next.

- Your people need feedback. Sharing with them what you notice in the moment is always useful, and if you are not leading the meeting, you're able to notice more.

MANAGERS

- Less-experienced employees need work on their process skills, so giving them responsibility for designing and leading your meeting is a way to build a core organizational competency.

- If you embrace the thinking that designing and leading meetings is a competency you want your people to have, then rotating the role among the group is useful. Be sure to work with them before and debrief with them after each meeting to maximize the value from the experience.

There also may be times when you would like everyone in your group to be able to focus on contributing to the conversation and not have to worry about leading or facilitating the conversation. Asking someone outside of your group and perhaps even outside of the organization can be helpful.

Master employee Q&A sessions

> "At the end of the day, I feel every single person has got to come away from a meeting with me with something positive.... My goal is that at every single session, people feel they've gained something from the experience."
>
> —Carlos Cantu, CEO, ServiceMaster

There is a more formal way to demonstrate your willingness to engage openly with employees, and that is with employee question-and-answer sessions. If you can master this conversation, you can change people's experience of working in an organization.

These sessions can be difficult, and sometimes you may wonder whether it's worth standing up in front of a large group of employees. But you most likely don't have time to reach everyone in smaller group conversations, and working with a group of seventy has more impact than sitting down with a group of seven.

MANAGERS

This is one time when the only practice you get is live. That's the bad news. The good news is that sincerity will carry the day, and with each session you offer, you'll move toward mastery.

An executive shared this story about her interactions with a group of factory employees:

> *Once a month, I do an update on how we are doing on quality targets. This last month, I did not have enough time to prepare the PowerPoint presentation that covers all data and results. So I just got up and talked to them about my impressions of how we were doing and where I thought we needed to focus. I spoke about what I thought they would like to know and what I wanted them to understand.*
>
> *Afterward, one of the wage employees caught up with me in the cafeteria and told me this. "Jill, you were wonderful this morning. I just felt like you were talking to us rather than giving us some prepared speech. And we all love listening to you because you just seem to care."*
>
> *It had never occurred to me that I could just do what I prefer to do anyway, which is simply talk to people.*

Q&A design

When you invite people to the session, let them know it is devoted to answering their questions and listening to their comments or concerns. You may find the first session goes slowly as people get familiar with this format, especially if they are used to PowerPoint presentations and information sharing.

Begin with yourself. Open the session by speaking with the group for four to eight minutes before asking for questions. This beginning conversation gives you a chance to connect by sharing about

If you have a guest speaker

If you have invited a senior staff member to speak to your group, ask the team to develop their questions in advance. Have at least ten questions prepared. Why? No questions at the end of a presentation can be interpreted as negative feedback, disengagement, or a lack of respect. This is not likely to be true, but having no questions asked can feel that way. One senior manager who spoke and received no questions afterward had these questions:

Wow, is it just a quiet group today?

Was my message appropriate?

Was I approachable enough?

Much better for the manager to be bombarded with authentic questions and leave with excitement and a feeling of the team's engagement.

yourself and what you've been doing. It also gives you a chance to warm up and allow the group to learn a bit more about you. There are three things you might talk about in this warm-up conversation:

- Share business news in which they might be interested.
- Tell them how you have been spending your time lately.
- Share conversations you've had with key customers, donors, suppliers, or organization executives. People love to be included in your conversations, even after the fact!

Let people know this is their session. Thank them in advance for their questions and comments. Let them know you are going to try to handle questions efficiently so a lot of questions can be covered during the session. Give people permission to keep asking until they get an answer. Let the group know you have someone taking notes for you, so if you promise you'll get back to them, they will know it has been noted.

Then open it up to their questions and comments. Let them know they can say or ask anything.

> *"What would you like to know? Please feel free to ask me anything about which you are interested, simply curious, or concerned."*

This is a rephrasing of coaching expert Tim Gallwey's question, which he designed to help people clear their minds before performing: *Is there anything at all about which you are curious, wondering, anxious, or concerned?*

Tim had this wonderful insight that whenever you are not at your best, there is simply a thought in the way. And if you can share that thought with someone else, you will be able to set it aside while you perform.

I was coaching a baseball team of thirteen- to fifteen-year-old boys when I first heard Tim talk about using this question to clear people before a presentation or test or competition. I decided to try it on the boys. The first couple of times, I didn't get a single response. The third time was different.

> ME: OK, boys, anything you want to ask about or are worried about?
>
> CATCHER: Can I play center field?
>
> ME: Talk to me—why are you asking?
>
> CATCHER: My dad is here, and he will stand behind the screen and yell at me after every pitch, and after about three innings, I'll start crying.

MANAGERS

ME: I'll ask your dad to sit by me.

CATCHER: He won't.

ME: We'll see.

Alas, his dad would not relent, figuring that I would not stand my ground because his kid was by far the best player and we needed him to be catching in order to win. His son played center field.

The next game, a small kid on the team asked if I would promise not to ask him to bunt during the game. I agreed after he promised to work on bunting during practice next week. He was relieved. About the seventh inning, he dropped down a perfect bunt. When he came to the dugout, I asked him why he bunted. "It just seemed like the right thing to do."

Giving people an opportunity to share whatever they are thinking gives them a chance to clear their minds so they can be at their best.

Wait for questions. The next step is to wait for someone to ask a question. Be careful not to make discounting comments such as "Surely someone has a question!" or "Who is brave enough to ask?" Your ability to tolerate silence and simply wait is important. Do not call on people in this setting, as it will put people on edge. Just hang in there. Trust the audience to come up with the questions. Think carefully before using anonymous submissions or questions collected before the session. Your intent is to demonstrate powerfully that people can speak up and it will work out.

Another option is to start by answering one or two questions you know are likely to be in the room—especially questions you think would demonstrate that anything is all right to ask.

MANAGERS

> **Q&A sessions are for the audience**—not the presenter—and to have the right mindset is critical. Listen to what is being said, because there is a real issue or opportunity being offered, and if you don't really listen, you will miss it. Most of the time people are sharing the issue because they care and really only want to know if you do also! Be calm, keep a positive perspective, and energize the audience. It has always amazed me how much better a team can function when they know you care.
>
> —R. David DeVault, Factory Manager, Fortune 100 company

Use people's names. When a hand is raised, call the person by name. If you don't know everyone's names, ask. People understand that you may not know everyone. They also understand if you can't remember. Once again, being sincere and honest works.

Listen carefully. Listen intently until they finish with their question or comment, then check for clarity if you aren't sure you understood.

Respond concisely. This session is designed to address as many questions as you can, so focus on being concise. It is critical to treat each question seriously and thoroughly, but be careful about long answers. When you've finished responding, check back to see if you've answered the question to the employee's satisfaction.

Not every question must be answered on the spot, but before you move on, let people know when they can expect a response. You have a wide range of options for replying to a comment or question.

When a comment doesn't require a response:

> *"Thank you, I appreciate knowing that."*
>
> *"I appreciate the comment, but I'm not going to do anything. Here's why. . . . Now where does that leave us? Are you OK with that?"*

MANAGERS

When a question doesn't appear on the surface to require a response:

> *"Do you have a request for me?"*

> *"Is there a question in there for me? It's OK if there isn't. I just didn't hear clearly what it was."*

When an answer is not readily available:

> *"Thanks for the question. I'm not sure I can answer it fully, but I'll tell you what I know."*

> *"I don't know the answer. I will find out and get back to you by Friday."*

> *"I would need to think about that. Let me get back to you by..."* (indicate time and method)

> *"Is this something you want me to answer now? Or do you want me to be thinking about it?"*

If you need more background information before responding:

> *"I'm not clear what you are asking; could you tell me more?"*

> *"Can you give me a little history on this?"*

You may also get asked questions you are unwilling to answer. The following are authentic options for responding:

> *"I could answer the question, but prefer to wait until..."*

> *"I'm sorry, but I'm unwilling to discuss this issue for reasons I cannot explain. I know you'd like to know more, but I am not willing to say more at this time. Thank you for the question and for respecting my preference not to answer."*

Acknowledge the comment or question if it really strikes a chord with you or gives you new insights or perspectives. Thank each person for participating before you move on to the next.

MANAGERS

In pursuit of clarity

During a question-and-answer session, a new factory manager was asked about his early impressions of being in the factory. He paused and then responded in a caring, wondering way: "Good question, and I'm still sorting it out, but two things come to mind: There isn't any warmth, and there seems to be so much noise."

It was a compelling moment because people realized that this manager was interested in how the factory felt as a place of work. The language was also memorable, which is one way to speak with impact.

After the manager left, the group discussed the value they were taking away from the Q&A session. The remarks about the lack of warmth and way too much noise resonated with almost everyone. As the conversation continued, they realized they did not know what the factory manager meant or what he was referring to.

The group could have taken the conversation to another level if someone had asked the manager to say more about his comments regarding warmth and noise. Great conversation is a two-way street.

Offer information readily. Part of building trust is to value transparency, and one powerful way to do that is to share information you think people would like to know but haven't specifically asked for. Don't make people ask the perfect question to get access to what you know.

Close the session. Thank people for attending and participating. If appropriate, review the list of commitments you've made. Give several examples of value you gained and what you learned from the session. Invite people to communicate with you in other ways if questions come up for them later or if there is something they would like you to know. Hang around to meet people and talk informally, ideally until there is no one left waiting to speak with you.

Ten mistakes executives make in Q&A sessions

1. Talking too long in the opening remarks
2. Not answering the question asked
3. Giving lengthy answers
4. Using humor inappropriately
5. Giving broad, philosophical answers rather than direct ones
6. Not checking back with the person who asked the question to see if it has been answered
7. Letting a conversation stay too long on one subject
8. Not making clear commitments when warranted
9. Not being genuine; not being yourself
10. Not enjoying people or seeing the value in conversation and learning

"Employees who believe that management is concerned about them as a whole person—not just an employee—are more productive, more satisfied, more fulfilled."

—Anne M. Mulcahy, former chairperson and CEO of Xerox

MANAGERS

Adopt an empowering perspective about complaints

Surfacing and working through complaints is part of having a great organization. When people realize they can complain and be heard, they begin to surface issues that need to be addressed.

At times, life stops working the way we want it to. Each of us has had complaints about a supervisor, our colleagues, or even family members. Good, loyal people complain.

In the work setting, good managers create an environment in which people feel safe to question, speak up, and, yes, even complain. In fact, people who are willing to speak up about something that is not working for them are a gift to the organization. If you aren't aware of a problem, you can't do anything to resolve it.

Try to resist the natural urge to get frustrated or defensive if people complain to you. Worry instead about people who have issues and say nothing. The alternatives to not complaining to you are whining to each other or keeping quiet out of hopelessness or apathy, and those alternatives are most likely worse for your organization.

The key idea here is that behind every complaint is a request. The task is to hear people out, then ask what they want—what is the request at the heart of the issue they're complaining about? For example:

> COMPLAINT: What happened as a result of the last employee survey? I know you want our input, but it doesn't seem as if the survey changes anything.

> UNDERLYING REQUEST: We would appreciate knowing the process for working with the results of the survey and getting a specific list of actions you intend to take as a result.

MANAGERS

If people can clearly state a concern or complaint and what they feel will resolve it, then you can begin to address the issue. Being able to listen and respond to complaints is a critical skill for supervisors—actually for anyone going through life!

Here are some reminders for when you respond to complaints:

- People take things personally, so go gently.
- Be supportive, even if the complaint seems unfounded or petty.
- Don't take the complaint personally or resist what they're saying.
- Don't justify or explain unless you are asked for an explanation.
- Go slowly (speak, listen, then listen some more) and trust that the conversation will work out.

Process steps: Listen and respond to complaints

This process begins with the person who has the complaint (a situation or behavior that does not work for them) stating the complaint and explaining so everyone is clear. Then the manager asks for the request behind the complaint—what the employee wants that would resolve it.

This is what it looks like as a series of process steps:

1. Manager: *"Thank you for bringing this issue to my attention. Tell me your concerns.*
2. Employee with complaint expresses the concern fully.
3. Manager just listens, asking questions only for clarity and understanding, then asks: *"Is there anything else?"*
4. Once the complaint has been expressed and understood, the manager asks the employee: *"What will resolve this for you?"* or *"What is your request?"*
5. Employee then asks for what he or she wants: *"Please do this for me"* or *"I just needed to express this. Thanks for listening to me."*

MANAGERS

6. Manager accepts the request or makes counter-offers until agreement is reached.

7. Employee acknowledges manager: *"Thanks for supporting me."*

If you think about it, most of the problems people have with one another are actually complaints. For example, you can probably think of times when your supervisor or a member of your team did something that didn't work for you, and you were frustrated, maybe even offended, by their demeanor. If you can express your concern (complaint) clearly and work through it as soon as possible (and not let it fester), then the concern will be addressed before it becomes a larger issue. It's often a matter of deciding to pay now by having that difficult conversation in a timely manner rather than pay a lot more later after the concern has grown or the parties have dug in their heels.

Like most managers, I imagine, I had this dream about being the best supervisor ever to work for. Then over time, that dream gets beaten down, and we end up settling for less. **Being a supervisor is tough. Let's acknowledge that, then get back to mastering the conversations that will make our dreams possible.**

TRY THIS

☐ Find a way to remind yourself that you matter to others.

☐ Slow down and acknowledge people you meet.

☐ Ask people for input (*What do you think?*) and where they stand on issues (*Where are you with this?*).

☐ For the next week, acknowledge a presenter in every meeting by sharing what you are taking away from his or her remarks.

MANAGERS

Before you disagree...

At times people will make comments with which you disagree. Be thoughtful before you respond. Often disagreeing will be seen as resistance to what they are saying. Your purpose in Q&A sessions and listening to complaints is to gain understanding and give people a chance to be heard.

When you feel yourself resisting, ask yourself, *Do I need to disagree here or simply listen?* Sometimes doing nothing with what is being said is the right move. *"Thank you for telling me. I appreciate the feedback."*

Other times, responding with a both/and approach is best. *"Your point is clear, and I see it a bit differently. May I tell you how I see it?"*

This is a way of acknowledging the other person's point of view while adding your own.

These practices make a difference when you need to respond to difficult comments:

- Assume positive intent.

- Take care of the people who are complaining.

- Just listen and get clear about the situation.

- Be sure their views have been fully expressed, and let them know you understood what they said.

- Make a thoughtful response that respects the person speaking.

- Take your time.

- Be the kind of person who is great to talk to.

MANAGERS

" You learn how to do life
by doing it.
You learn more slowly if you think
you can skip this part. "

—Brian Andreas
American author

"Learn to communicate so your players feel more capable, valuable and loved. You must see capability when there is no evidence...see value when there is evidence to the contrary...and see what's lovable even when it's hard to find."

—Tim Gallwey
The Inner Game of Tennis

Dealing with
Ineffective Behavior
in Meetings

Core ideas:

- People are great . . . and sometimes difficult.
- Choose an empowering perspective: Assume positive intent.
  - Up-front agreements provide the framework for difficult conversations.
  - Is the behavior a singular event or a pattern?
- Three options for responding to behavior that doesn't work:
  - Let it go and make it work.
  - Stop the behavior in the moment and ask for what you want.
  - Speak with the person away from the group setting.
- Conducting difficult conversations is worth the effort.

"What you are afraid to do
is a clear indication
of the next thing
you need to do."

—Eleanor Roosevelt
First Lady

People are great…and sometimes difficult

Once you take on improving your meetings, you will be faced with behavior that doesn't work, and you'll need to decide what, if anything, you will do about it. The intent here is to review the underlying principles and ideas for dealing with ineffective behavior and provide enough examples so you can then map the ideas onto your own situation.

It's not possible to prescribe a perfect answer, since all situations are unique. There are entire books written on dealing with difficult people. My intent here is to apply the essential message of this book—that conversation and relationship are the foundation for getting things done—to the issue of behavior. In the spirit of taking care of people, consider talking with them about behavior that either erodes the effectiveness of the meeting or damages the reputation of the individual with the behavior. The examples are provided to give you a sense of how the ideas would sound if applied. Certainly there are many more situations than what is covered here.

These are the most frequently expressed behavioral issues:

- How do I deal with the person who interrupts and speaks over me and others in meetings?

- How do I deal with people who jump into every conversation and speak more often than they should?

- How do I handle the person who makes outlandish, negative remarks in our meetings?

- How do I handle the person who makes inappropriate comments?

- How do I handle people who don't keep their word?

I recall having the following conversation with my boss, Bill:

> BILL: Paul, have you noticed that whenever Pete speaks in a meeting, he just goes on and on and on?
>
> ME: Yes.
>
> BILL: I want you to talk to him and get him to stop doing it.
>
> ME: But, he works for you.
>
> BILL: Exactly, and I don't want to make it more significant than it is. So you are going to handle it.
>
> ME: OK.

So I invited Pete to coffee, and this is how our conversation went:

> ME: Pete, you are probably aware of this, but I've noticed that you continue speaking after you've made your point in meetings. You may not be aware that it has become a pattern, and that people are not paying close attention to what you are saying anymore. I think you should do something about it.
>
> PETE: I know, I know. I just get going and can't find a way to stop.

Pete and I then agreed that in every meeting, I would sit directly across from him, and once he had made his point, I would give him a very subtle indication that he needed to wrap up. At first, the best he could do was an abrupt, "I'm done." But over time, he began to speak much more concisely and conclude his point more naturally.

There were three lessons in this experience for me.

- Most people are aware of what they do that is difficult for others.

- People prefer to be told, and it's a gift when we do tell them.

- Awareness is the first step toward changing behavior.

Knowing they have an ineffective behavioral pattern does not mean they are aware of it in the moment or that they are in touch with the price they pay by continuing to do it. When you talk to them about it, it's a chance to start anew.

If you have your heart in the right place when you talk to someone, the conversation will work out. In any case, remember to trust your instincts and do what seems to fit for you.

Remember, people are people

One of my mentors consistently reminded managers: "Everyone is a little bit scared and a whole lot proud. And if you remember this, you'll be better with people."

You've also heard the phrase, "It's nothing personal—it's just business." The only problem with this phrase is that, if there is a person involved, it is personal.

In meetings, you can put this perspective into action when you:

- acknowledge people when they enter the room.
- check in with people a few minutes before and after the meeting.
- give people your complete attention when they speak during the meeting.
- acknowledge when someone's comments add to your thinking.
- speak respectfully when you disagree.
- notice who hasn't spoken yet and invite them into the conversation.
- walk in with the presumption that everyone in the room has good intentions.

Choose an empowering perspective: Assume positive intent

You and I sometimes do things that don't work for others. Whether at home or at work, if we are honest, we realize that we can be difficult to live with or work with at times. Staying in touch with our own ways of being difficult can help serve as a reminder to give others a break. Good people behave in difficult ways for lots of reasons. Why they do it is less important than the effect their behavior has on your meetings. But it is useful to remember that people do not plot out on their way to work how best to sabotage your meeting. It is not intentional.

So let's start by giving everyone the benefit of the doubt. Assume their intentions are good. We do this for ourselves, so let's just extend the same courtesy to others.

Also, set high standards for how to deal with people when they are being a bit difficult. Respond in a way that the other person will appreciate and those watching will respect. Avoid doing anything that, upon later reflection, you might wish you hadn't done.

Up-front agreements provide the framework for difficult conversations

Agreements are designed to address patterns of behavior you can expect to run into when working with other people. Agreements are covered in strategies 3, 6, and 8, but if the leader doesn't review them in the opening for the meeting, they might not be much help. The old saying "Out of sight, out of mind" applies to agreements. If you review your working agreements at the beginning of each meeting, you will have less behavior to deal with and more permission to bring it up when you do.

BEHAVIOR

Is the behavior a singular event or a pattern?

A fundamental question is whether you're looking at a singular event or a pattern of behavior. There are certain behaviors for which organizations have decided they are not waiting for a pattern. Instead, they have adopted a "zero tolerance" approach—sexual harassment, for example, or illegal or unethical practices.

Most meeting behaviors are not of the "zero tolerance" category. Occasional events, such as a cell phone ringing or someone having a side conversation, can just be overlooked. If these events become a pattern, then they are distracting and need to be addressed.

Three options for responding to behaviors that don't work

Within the context of meetings, you can use this model to help decide what, if anything, you will do. In dealing with behavior that doesn't work in meetings, you have three options for responding.

Option 1: Let it go and make it work without taking it on. You simply wait for the behavior to stop, then restart as though it didn't happen. This often is the best move because it is the most comfortable for everyone and least confronting. The downside, of course, is that the behavior goes unchallenged and perhaps unnoticed, and sometimes the quality of the group conversation suffers as a result.

Option 2: Stop the behavior in the moment and ask for what you want. This is a bit confronting, but it does lessen the impact of the behavior. It also allows you to take a stand for best conversational practices. The trick is to do this in a way that doesn't make someone wrong or upset the group conversation. Your intention to be supportive and your tone of voice are important. You might also try saying, *"Tell me more about what you are thinking."* It's confronting, but in a positive, supportive way.

Option 3: Speak with the person away from the group setting. After the meeting, let the individual know that the behavior was distracting, disempowering, and costly to you and the group. This is the most confronting of the three options, but it is the most likely option for producing a long-term change in the behavior.

Let's look at how each of these options might sound when dealing with typical complaints experienced in meetings.

How do I deal with the person who interrupts and speaks over me and others in meetings?

Option 1: Let it go and make it work. Let the person who interrupts finish his or her comments, then finish what you were saying or ask the person who was interrupted to finish his or her remarks. You can do this both as the person leading the meeting or as a participant.

> *"Sarah, I'm not sure you had a chance to finish your comments. Would you please make your points again?"*

Option 2: Stop the interruption and ask for what you want.

> *"Todd, I wasn't quite finished. I'd like to finish and then I'd love to hear your thoughts."*

> *"Todd, I'd like to hold you back for a moment while Sarah finishes her thoughts. Thank you."*

Option 3: Speak with the person away from the meeting.

> *"Todd, I appreciate your willingness to participate in the group conversations. It would be helpful to me and to the group, however, if you pulled back about 15 percent, spoke a bit less, and also interrupted less. Does this make sense to you?"*

How do I deal with people who jump into every conversation and speak more often than they should?

Option 1: Let it go and make it work. Simply listen intently each time they speak and let them finish. It's easy to become judgmental, but if you're unwilling to say anything, your focus needs to be on finding value in what they are saying. Tough, I know, but doable.

You can also manage this indirectly by asking three people to begin each conversation. By calling on three people who tend not to jump into the conversation quickly, you are changing the pattern of the group. You can also call on the person who jumps in so he or she knows there will be an opportunity to get into the conversation, but more on your terms.

Option 2: Stop the behavior and ask for what you want.

> "Frank, if you don't mind, I'd like to hold you back for a bit while I get a couple of other people into the conversation."

Option 3: Speak with the person away from the meeting.

> "Frank, I would like the participation levels to be a bit more balanced in our meetings. To achieve this, it would be helpful if you waited until other people entered the conversation on some topics before you did. Also, I would appreciate if you would look for who might like to get into the conversation and invite them in."

How do I handle the person who makes outlandish, negative remarks in our meetings?

Option 1: Ignore it and get back to the intended conversation. As a single occurrence, it's not an issue. People have bad days. If it is a pattern, you can't ignore comments that erode the group's ability to feel safe, enjoy the conversation, and be productive. Plus, group members will eventually lose respect for the person.

BEHAVIOR

Option 2: Stop the behavior in the moment and ask for what you want. You have a series of options here depending on how confronting you would like to be:

"Jim, I'm not sure what to do with what you just said."

"Jim, I don't think your comments are useful. Do you?"

"Jim, what are you intending to accomplish with your comments?"

Option 3: Speak with the person away from the meeting. Let the person know you don't think that it helps the conversation or the group when he or she makes comments that seem random, negative, or discounting. You can also say how difficult such comments make it for you to manage the conversation.

"Jim, I just want you to be aware that your negative remarks detract from the meeting. I also don't think you want people to associate such remarks with you because eventually people will lose respect for you. Please take a look at this."

How do I handle the person who makes inappropriate comments during meetings?

Learn to recognize when someone's comments are discounting or inappropriate and address it when it happens. Disparaging remarks about a person's gender, racially derogatory remarks, verbal abuse, suggestive remarks, belittling someone's accent—these aren't appropriate anywhere, but especially not in the workplace. If a conversation seems "off" to you, don't let it go by.

Option 1: This not a viable option if the behavior is truly inappropriate.

Option 2: Treat the comment seriously. Don't ignore it or let it go. This will let people know that they just can't go around saying things when you are managing the conversation. Use any one of the following:

"What do you want us to do with what you just said?"

"I think you're better than that comment might suggest. Can we keep things more professional and courteous please?"

"I consider what you just said to be inappropriate. There simply isn't a place for those remarks in this group or in this organization."

Stay in the conversation until you feel it's been addressed or the other person has said something that allows you to move on.

The caution here and in many of these situations is to handle the issue in a way that everyone in the group admires how you addressed it. If you make a mistake in how you react, apologize to the person and the group. We've all been there. It takes a committed person to speak up, and it takes a big person to apologize when we don't get it right.

Option 3: Explain in clear, direct terms that the remarks are inappropriate.

"Jim, your remarks were insensitive and unacceptable. I will review your comments with HR later today and meet with you again tomorrow morning."

How do I handle people who don't keep their word?

Option 1: This time letting it go means not commenting on the lack of delivery. Simply ask the person for a new completion date. If this is a single event, this is the best option. We all don't keep our word at times, but a pattern of nondelivery needs intervention.

"Bill, by when can you complete this task?"

Also, consider what you can do in future to reduce the number of times team members don't keep their word. When you create commitments:

- Be specific about what you asking for by when.
- Ask if the due date works for them.
- Let them know you're counting on them; ask if they need support.

- Discuss whether you will check in with each other along the way.

- Make sure the commitments are written and visible somewhere.

Option 2: If using option 1 fails repeatedly, then consider saying something more direct.

> *"Bill, I expect there is a good reason, but next time, please call and let me know if you're not going to meet a deadline."*

If you've done all this, then look for an opportunity to ask what is going on, because you want to be reliable with each other.

Option 3: Get across that nondelivery is unacceptable. While you want to be understanding of their circumstances, they need to understand that not doing what they say they will do simply doesn't work. Candidly expressing both your disappointment and your expectations is often all you can do.

> *"Bill, I know we've been clear about the importance of keeping the commitments we make. Please do what you need to do to be more reliable in the future."*

Then, make it a point to follow up closely on all future commitments. Following up consistently is time-consuming but effective.

Conducting difficult conversations is worth the effort

Dealing with ineffective behavior in meetings falls into the overall theme of conducting difficult conversations. This additional background will be useful should you choose to speak with people away from the meeting.

Some conversations are difficult because they don't work out well when we try to have them. Others seem so difficult that we avoid having them—we think about having them, but we don't.

There are lots of reasons we don't have these conversations. First, we don't want to be uncomfortable ourselves, and we see the potential for someone being upset and the situation getting worse. We try to persuade ourselves that their behavior is not a big deal. We also avoid difficult conversations because we simply don't know how to make them work. These explanations allow us to get away with not having the conversation.

Second, we are not aware of the downstream costs we incur by not voicing our concerns. If we were in touch with the price we ultimately pay, we'd have the conversations. Sometimes the price is that the situation gets worse. An even bigger price is losing out on something special that might be possible if we immediately handled these issues.

Ever say to yourself, "Why did I wait so long?" Sometimes, doing whatever we'd been putting off doesn't turn out to be so difficult after all. Sometimes we get access to something much more exciting having done whatever we were avoiding.

That's the way it is with difficult conversations. It's always different on the other side—once you've had the conversation. And it is possible to design the conversation so that it works for everyone.

The first step is to sit down and think through the conversation and how you want it to go.

Don't have the conversation unless you are committed to the person, are willing to stay with the conversation until it works out for the other person, and are clear that you are building something by raising this issue.

BEHAVIOR

Think about but don't be stopped by these questions:

- *When would this conversation work best for the other person?*
- *Is this a group issue or an individual issue?*
- *Am I in the right frame of mind to have this conversation?*
- *Am I willing to do whatever it takes, even if the other person isn't?*

Get in touch with how you'd like to be approached if someone has something to say that you're likely to take personally and get defensive about. When you start the conversation, here are the steps to take:

1. Let them know why you want to have the conversation. Tell them that something is not working for you, and ask for permission to explain. Explain what is important to you that is being put in jeopardy. Use facts. Be specific.

2. Let them know that this is a problem for you and acknowledge that it may not be an issue for them. Share that this is your perception of the problem—it may not be the truth. Ask them to share their view of it. Listen intently and let them know that you fully heard what they said.

3. Take care of them. Let them know you value them and the relationship. If you are concerned about causing damage to the relationship by raising this issue, tell them. Share your thinking with them. Remind them that you want to stay with this conversation until it works for both of you.

4. If you have other concerns, share those also. Voicing concerns both gives you freedom and lets them know you care and want this to work. It also lessens the chance your fears will materialize.

5. Acknowledge any concerns you think they may have.

6. If you have a request, make it. If you don't know what to do, let them know. Ask them what they see to do about it.

7. Give them permission not to respond immediately or even during this conversation.

BEHAVIOR

8. Before you end the conversation, decide what the next steps are. When will you talk about it again? How will you continue to work on this? How will you know when it is no longer an issue for either of you?

9. Let them know you appreciate being able to talk to them.

You may never be comfortable having these conversations. With practice, you can become effective in having them. That's what counts.

Think it through beforehand

Use these questions to help prepare for having a difficult conversation.

- What is the issue to talk about?
- Why does it need to be discussed?
- What do you want as outcomes?
- Look at current cost versus long-term cost or lost potential.
- What are you worried might happen if you bring it up?
- What should you include in the conversation so it works for them, for you, and afterward?
- What should you avoid doing or saying?
- What should you avoid reacting to?
- What do you want to focus on during the conversation?

TRY THIS

☐ For two weeks, assume positive intent for every action and comment with which you disagree. See whether your responses change.

☐ Identify agreements that would make things easier if you put them into practice.

☐ Invite someone to coffee you wouldn't normally invite.

BEHAVIOR

" Everyone designs who devises courses of action aimed at changing existing situations into preferred ones. "

—Herbert Simon
American scientist

Appendix A
Tailored Designs

The following designs have proved useful over time. In fact, these designs are the "best of the best" from over thirty-five years of designing retreats and working with groups.

Still, remember that a design is intended to inform and guide, not constrain and control. Give yourself permission to edit, adapt, and play with different approaches. Always trust yourself and your group—you know what will work for your people.

Setting goals : Determine your focus for the year

When working with teams, this series of questions has proved effective in determining what goals they wish to set for the year. The team develops a list for each question, then chooses the final goals from the entire set of lists. The primary purpose of this conversation is to explore what else you might choose to take on beyond what you have been asked to produce. Not because you have so much free time. Not because you aren't already doing enough. But because there might be a richer set of possibilities available if you were to decide to change your focus for the year. The point is to continue to be thoughtful and open to something different.

The secondary outcome of this conversation is to be aligned as a group about where you need to focus your efforts.

Process steps:

- *What have we specifically been asked to produce by the organization or our customers and stakeholders?*
- *What is expected even though no one has asked?*
- *What else do we know we could do and no one is asking us?*
- *What do we think we might be able to do but can't guarantee?*
- *On our best days, what do we sometimes allow ourselves to dream about doing?*
- *Now, given everything we have listed, what is it we will publicly commit to doing this year?*

Starting the day: The daily start-up meeting

One of the most productive meetings is the daily start-up meeting for a new project or for a maintenance turnaround in a factory. This meeting is focused on one thing—getting clarity about what needs to get done that day.

Process steps:

- *What do we need to accomplish today?*
- *Anything happen yesterday we need to discuss and act upon?*
- *Anyone need any help?*
- *Anything everyone needs to be aware of or watch out for today?*
- *OK, everyone clear about our assignments?*
- *Remember to call if something happens that you didn't expect or if one of your action items gets in danger of not being finished.*

Depending on the size and scope of the project, these meetings can last from fifteen to forty-five minutes. If longer than fifteen, release people as soon as they have their marching orders for the day. The focus is to get in, have the conversations necessary to gain clarity for the day, and get out.

Checking in with your group

The intent behind this conversation is to find out how everyone is doing and perhaps surface issues that need to be addressed.

Depending on the size of the group and how much there is to talk about, this can be somewhere between a twenty- to sixty-minute conversation. Listen for when the conversation begins to run out of energy, then wrap up using the five pieces of closure: completion, alignment, commitment, value, and appreciation.

This is how the setup might sound:

> *"My intention here is to have an open-ended conversation about where we are, how we are doing, where we're going as an organization, and what we need to focus on right now. What is important is that you share what you are thinking and feeling. Let's have this be a free and open dialogue and not be worried about getting to a specific outcome. If there are other questions or places you would like to take the conversation, that is fine also."*

Process steps:

- *Here's where we are going as an organization.*
- *Here's where we need to focus right now.*
- *What support do you need for your work?*
- *What support do you need personally?*
- *Is there anything you'd like to know or ask me about?*

Gathering input from your group

The intent of this conversation is for people to provide input to you in an informal yet powerful format. The value is partly in what input is received and partly in being given the invitation to speak.

This conversation allows a group to discuss and recommend where you might focus more time and energy. Doing this with your group directly is more powerful than asking for anonymous feedback. It also demonstrates how an open, candid culture should operate.

If you have this conversation within the structure of a meeting, don't spend more than twenty or thirty minutes on it. Over coffee, you can take up to an hour. Feel free to take notes.

The setup might sound something like this:

> *"Thank you for being willing to do this. I would love to listen to the group have a conversation about where I should focus or put my attention in the next year. After working together, you know where I spend my time, and you know what I pay attention to. I want to get better. I always want to get better. So where do you think I could make more of a difference to you and the organization if I thought more about or focused my time on something?"*

> Or: *"What is it that influences the character and identity of this organization and therefore should guide what I pay attention to? I'm not looking for an answer or a list of things to do. I'm looking for whatever insight or awareness that this conversation might bring to me and to you. I'm also going to try to just listen, so I'm going to ask to manage the conversation so everyone gets a chance and so we don't get bogged down."*

Process steps:

1. Put people into groups of three or four and give them ten minutes to discuss what they might want to express. Be clear that this first ten minutes is a process step intended to give everyone time to get into the conversation. It's not about creating team reports. When the whole group conversation begins, you want everyone to shift back to speaking as individuals who have ownership for their remarks.

2. *What thoughts do you have for me?*

3. *What specific requests do you have for me?*

4. Wrap up by sharing four or five points you are taking away from the conversation.

Reviewing accomplishments

The purpose of this conversation is to establish a context of accomplishment and fulfillment for the group. This conversation is also an opportunity for people to acknowledge the work of others and even their own.

There is always more work to be done in an organization. There are always new goals and difficult issues with which to deal. There never seems to be a break in the action or a time to stop and feel good about what you've done together. This is a time where you stop and remind yourselves about what you have accomplished in the last three, six, or twelve months.

Set aside thirty minutes so there is no need to feel rushed. Ask people to consider three perspectives: One that reflects the accomplishment of the group, one that reflects the accomplishment of a colleague, and one that reflects something they are proud of as their own accomplishment. Acknowledge up front that many people have been raised not to pat ourselves on the back. Simply ask people to set that aside for this conversation as it's important in terms of knowing each other and to develop a sense of what we value in our own work.

Process steps:

1. Begin with these broad questions:
   - *What should we be very proud of?*
   - *What have we produced, discovered, or made possible?*
   - *Where and with whom have we made a difference?*
   - *Individually and collectively, what should we feel good about?*

2. Then expand the range of items that might be included far beyond the narrow way we tend to think of accomplishment.

You might prepare a handout so people can refer to these throughout the conversation:

- *What have we made possible that wasn't before?*
- *What new thinking do we have?*
- *What new systems and structures have we created?*
- *What have we learned? How are we different?*
- *What limits and problems have we uncovered?*
- *What would our stakeholders say we have accomplished?*
- *What new capabilities do we have as individuals; as an organization?*
- *How have we improved how we work together?*

3. Closure: As leader, make notes and comment on a few at the end that resonated with you. Invite three or four people to share what value they are taking away from the conversation.

Getting feedback from your peers

It's important to know how we come across to others. The purpose of this conversation is to create an easy way for people to help you determine where some renewed awareness or attention would make a difference to their experience of interacting with you.

This is best handled in groups of three or four with people who work closely together. A small group is surprisingly safer and more impactful at the same time than one-on-one feedback. Plus, it gives people who are not speaking time to reflect and find other things to share.

Process steps:

1. Group selects assessment tools or checklists to review and identify feedback points; see appendix B.

2. Each person in the group receives feedback for fifteen minutes. One of the people giving feedback begins by finding three points from the tool or checklist to share about the person receiving feedback. The other two members of the group can then add their points. It's a relaxed conversation with everyone looking for what might make a difference to the person receiving the feedback.

   The person receiving feedback listens to each person, asking questions only for clarity or acknowledging what is said. Acknowledgment doesn't imply agreement or that the recipient plans to do anything with the feedback. It just means the person follows what is being said.

3. After fifteen minutes, switch to the next person. After everyone has received feedback, then everyone shares what they are taking away from the conversation.

Two strategies for learning from colleagues

Seeking input from colleagues

Seeking input from colleagues is a typical approach to group problem solving, where someone describes a situation and then everyone participates in exploring it. This is different from a back-and-forth problem-solving conversation.

Process steps:

1. Presenting member shares the idea or situation for five to eight minutes.

2. Group asks clarifying questions.

3. The entire group shares reactions, ideas, and potential concerns. Presenting member just listens or asks clarifying questions.

4. Presenting member summarizes the conversation and makes suggestions about where he or she still needs the thinking of the group.

5. Entire group continues to think together.

6. Presenting member thanks the group and shares what he or she is taking away from the conversation.

Roundtable discussion

Gwil Evans of Oregon State University and I have worked on the design of many large meetings and retreats. We share an expression—the best part of any retreat is "driving out of the parking lot."

Here's a note I received from Gwil about an innovative design that allows a group to "eavesdrop" on a small-group conversation before opening the discussion to the full group:

> *Thought of you when I was driving out of the parking lot after a successful Administrators' Workshop that spanned parts of three days. As design goes, most of the sessions were a fairly traditional exchange of information. My favorite, however, was set up as a small round table up on the riser, with tablecloth and unobtrusive microphones. At the table, we convened two of our department heads, both of whom are considering adopting a 'school' model for organizing a program in their spheres of responsibility. They were joined by two other faculty, both of whom now already head schools. We set up the situation as an 'over coffee' conversation among the four of them, with the rest of us in the room 'eavesdropping' on their conversation about schools and what it takes to establish and operate them.*

> *The result was a kind of free-flowing exchange of ideas, pretty much what one would expect in a coffee shop. And content rich. Included occasional good humor (laughing at oneself, etc.). Then, after about thirty minutes, the rest of us 'dropped in' on the conversation and introduced our questions and ideas. Afterward, I received many independent thanks for the setup and approval for the design. Nice reward!*

This is a creative approach that has colleagues sharing views versus engaging in problem solving in a typical back-and-forth conversation.

Additional process steps for designing conversations

The following are additional questions to consider when mapping out the process steps for various conversation designs. You may wish to tailor the six basic designs that are described in the design chapter.

Analyzing a situation:
- What's the situation?
- What do we know about this?
- What else is included in this?
- What are all the themes here?
- Any other views or perspectives to consider?
- What information do we need?
- How should we work on these?
- What options do we have?
- What are the threats or opportunities of each option?

Reaching for alignment:
- Here's what I'd like to do.
- What questions do you have?
- Is this clear?
- Does it make sense?
- Do you see the value in it?
- What do you need to align with this?
- Is there anything in your way?
- Is there anything missing that you need?
- Any showstoppers for you?
- Can everyone live with this?
- Can you support this?

Making a decision:
- What decision process will we use?
- Whose decision is it?
- Who needs to be involved or consulted?
- Who has veto power?
- What are the objectives?
- What are the decision criteria?
- What are the alternatives?
- What are the associated benefits and risks?
- What is the best decision?
- What could go wrong?
- How can we prevent it?
- What can go right?
- How can we maximize it?
- Are we vulnerable in any way?
- Will this decision limit us in the future?
- How will we communicate this to others?

Creating a goal:
- What have we been asked to produce?
- What is expected of us?

- What difference do we want to make?
- What do we know is possible?
- What do we think might be possible?
- What are we willing to guarantee?
- What are we willing to go for?
- What will we publicly commit to?

Checking for completion:

- What else about this?
- Is there anything that hasn't been said?
- Is there anything that you are curious about?
- Are there any concerns or worries?
- Everyone ready to move on?
- Is there anything you need to say or ask?

Checking in with people:

- Where are you with this?
- Is this clear?
- Are there any questions about this?
- Reactions, thoughts, ideas?
- What do you think?

Summarizing and next steps:

- So, where are we?
- Can we summarize this?
- Where do we go from here?
- What are the next steps?
- What are the next milestones?
- Who will do what by when?
- Who will track this for us?
- Do we need ongoing meetings?
- Who needs to be included or informed?

"A human moment occurs when two or more people are together, paying attention to one another."

—Edward M. Hallowell
American psychiatrist

Appendix B
Relationship-Building Exercises

If you are looking to create unity in a group, perhaps the most important way to do so is to get to know one another beyond what occurs as a result of working together. If you get to know one another, everything becomes easier.

Doing the following exercises will deepen the relationships in the group. In particular, the listening exercises will fundamentally change the way you interact in conversations and meetings.

One criteria I've always held to over the years is never ask a group of people to do something that I would not ask a group of CEOs to do. I remember being part of a state leadership initiative for high school seniors. The folks who organized the event began by having everyone throw their shoes into a pile, then asking each person to take two shoes and find the owners. There are simply much more powerful ways to connect people. Rely on your own sense of what would fit your group.

Listening exercise for individuals

This is a training tool to reacquaint people with the value of just listening. It usually is a bit awkward, or at least different, for people because it is a clear departure from the norm of talking back and forth. Some people whose natural preference is to be quiet will find it easy to listen for several minutes at a time but will find speaking at length more uncomfortable. Conversely, people who speak readily will be frustrated at not being allowed to ask questions or make comments as they listen. That's what this exercise is designed to disrupt.

Even though people will get the idea of it after one round, after five rounds, people will experience a profound change in how they listen.

Instructions:

Please find a partner and decide who will speak first, who will listen first, and which topic you will work on together. Partner with someone you do not know well.

When you are speaking, speak for the whole time you are given. It's fine to stop and start. When you are listening, just listen. Don't say anything. Don't worry about remembering what they say or formulating a response. Give them your full attention. Relax and enjoy the conversation.

Process steps:

1. Give people a couple of minutes to choose a topic from the lists below, then check to make sure everyone is ready to start. Ask them to begin, and start keeping track of time.

2. After 2.5 minutes, stop them and tell them to switch roles and let the other person speak on the same question for another 2.5 minutes.

3. After the second 2.5-minute period, tell them to take a minute or two to chat back and forth—to have a normal conversation.

4. After a couple more minutes, stop and debrief the group with these questions:

   "What are your observations about listening in this way?"

   "What are your observations about being listened to in this way?"

5. After debriefing for five to ten minutes, ask them to find new partners and choose a new question on which to speak.

Repeat this process for five rounds. Add to the length of the listening time by fifteen seconds in each round.

Topics:

1. Tell me about your family.

2. Tell me about the neighborhood in which you grew up.

3. How did you come to be at this place in your career?

4. What are your outside interests, and how did you come to have them?

5. What do you remember from your childhood (favorite room, toys, friends, memories)?

6. What is your story?

7. Tell me about a current project about which you are excited.

8. Tell me about a part of work where you are not making the progress you want.

9. What are you currently facing at work and home? What's your current reality?

10. What can you tell me about yourself that I might be interested in knowing?

11. When you are in a group, what value do you try to add?

12. What experiences or people have influenced you?

13. What has become clear to you about yourself or life recently?

14. What possibilities are associated with how you are spending your time?

15. Where would you like to be in five to ten years both personally and professionally?

16. What do you worry about?

17. What do you hold dear in your life?

Listening exercise for groups

This version of the exercise allows a small group of people to deepen their relationships by working through a series of conversations together. Something magical happens when a group has the opportunity to spend an hour sharing and listening to each other.

Process steps:

1. Follow the same speaking and listening instructions for individuals but with groups of four—put together a group where knowing more about each other would be useful to working together in the future.

2. There will be three rounds where each person speaks to a question for 2.5 minutes—each round takes ten minutes.

3. Choose three different topics. Each person speaks to the same topic in each round. Take your time. Relax. No place to get to—enjoy the conversation.

4. Reflect on the conversations and what you learned about members of your group with these questions:

"What observations do you have about this exercise either as a process or in terms of what happened?"

"What conversations would you like to follow up on in the future?"

Topics:

All of the questions in the previous exercise can be used in this exercise. In addition, you might like these:

1. What moments or experiences defined who you are today?

2. Tell me about a family member who brings out the best in you.

3. What difference would you like to make in the time you have left in your career?

4. What are you at work on in terms of personal development?

5. What impact do you see that your group might have on your organization?

6. How do you best relax, get away, and take care of yourself?

7. What do you want to be true in the future about your organization that is not true now?

What can I tell you?

Ask people to gather in groups of six, preferably with people they work with, but that is not necessary. Each person gets six minutes to answer this question:

> *"What can I tell you about myself that might make it easier to understand me and work with me?"*

Each person is timed, and no one else in the group is allowed to speak or ask questions. It's a bit like the practice of dialogue, where no one can get into a conversation until the speaker gives up the rock. Only here, the exercise is structured so that people keep looking for other things to say.

Doing this exercise in a nice environment, perhaps over wine or coffee, is wonderful as it allows for a more relaxed conversation. The intent is for a slow, no-place-to-get-to conversation with one person speaking and everyone else just listening.

As you can imagine, there are lots of ways to redesign this conversation depending on group preferences and the time you are willing to devote to this.

Just know the conversation always gets a group to a higher level of connection among individuals and across the group.

New supervisor connecting process

This is designed to essentially be an interview between a new supervisor and his or her group. It is valuable both for the learning that occurs, but also for the ongoing permission it establishes about asking questions and raising concerns.

1. As the supervisor, begin by answering this question for eight minutes:

   "What can I tell you about myself that might make it easier for you to understand me and work with me?"

2. After speaking to the first question for eight minutes, then open up the session to the group. Let the group know they can ask you anything.

   "What would you like to know about working with me?"

3. Ask everyone how they prefer to be supervised and interacted with.

4. Review a set of agreements for working together.

   "This is what I'd like to set up with you as a set of working agreements:

   - *Let's be clear about goals and expectations, and if either one of us feels we are not clear or sure, let's talk.*

   - *If you have anything at all about which you are curious, wondering, or concerned, please ask. I promise to tell you the truth.*

   - *If I have any concerns about your performance or if I hear of any from other people in the organization, I will tell you within a week.*

- *You have access to me at all times, and this is how you can reach me.*

- *You can ask or tell me anything, and I promise not to share it with anyone without your permission. Please recognize that there are certain things I must tell HR and other things I'm going to ask you to help me figure out what to do with.*

- *Let's have each other's back."*

5. Then thank the group and reemphasize the key points in how you would like to work with them in the future.

Sharing photographs to get to know each other

The purpose of this exercise is to continue to learn new things about people so that the level of connection with each other deepens. Everything about working together gets easier as you get to know each other in more ways. As Abraham Lincoln said, *"I don't like that man. I'm going to have to get to know him."*

This exercise is useful at a day-long meeting or retreat. Do this exercise fairly early so people can continue to ask others about their photos throughout the retreat. An extended first break is a good time to do this. Set aside forty-five minutes for both the exercise and a break.

Ask people to bring three to five photos about people and things that matter to them and that would be interesting to others. Photos that have stories behind them are wonderful, as are more historical photos. It works best if people bring hard copies rather than their smartphones since the photos can more easily be passed around.

Encourage people to find time during the retreat to see and hear about everyone's photos.

"A mentor long departed told me that the greatest gift in political life, in any life, is to view yourself objectively, at arm's length, to make an assessment of yourself."

—Hugh Carey
American politician

Appendix C
Assessment Tools

A ssessment tools are starting places—not final answers. They are snapshots that give us something from which to think and discuss. The tools included here do not necessarily relate directly to meetings, but the link is there.

Key project relationship assessment

Identify the ten relationships external to the project team that are critical to the success of your project. Then evaluate the key relationships on the basis of overall quality, level of trust, and knowledge of one another's interests, commitments, projects, and concerns.

Rating criteria:

Rate the *quality* of each relationship from one to ten. Compare each to the best working relationship you have in the organization, regardless of whether your best relationship is connected to this project or not. One is bad, ten is great. Ten means you can say anything to or ask anything of the other person easily.

Rate the amount of *trust* between you and the other person. Ten is trust completely both ways; one is no trust at all. If you can't give the relationship a ten, what is in the way or missing?

Rate how well you know the *other person's interests*, commitments, projects, and what they are facing.

Rate how well the other person knows your interests, commitments, and what you are facing.

PERSON A: Date of last conversation_____

Quality of relationship	1 2 3 4 5 6 7 8 9 10
Trust level	1 2 3 4 5 6 7 8 9 10
I know his or her reality	1 2 3 4 5 6 7 8 9 10
He or she knows mine	1 2 3 4 5 6 7 8 9 10

PERSON B: Date of last conversation_____

Quality of relationship	1 2 3 4 5 6 7 8 9 10
Trust level	1 2 3 4 5 6 7 8 9 10
I know his or her reality	1 2 3 4 5 6 7 8 9 10
He or she knows mine	1 2 3 4 5 6 7 8 9 10

PERSON C: Date of last conversation_____

Quality of relationship	1 2 3 4 5 6 7 8 9 10
Trust level	1 2 3 4 5 6 7 8 9 10
I know his or her reality	1 2 3 4 5 6 7 8 9 10
He or she knows mine	1 2 3 4 5 6 7 8 9 10

PERSON D: Date of last conversation_____

Quality of relationship	1 2 3 4 5 6 7 8 9 10
Trust level	1 2 3 4 5 6 7 8 9 10
I know his or her reality	1 2 3 4 5 6 7 8 9 10
He or she knows mine	1 2 3 4 5 6 7 8 9 10

Comments and next steps_____

APPENDIX C

Trust and respect assessment

Someone once said that brilliance is in the details. What specific, day-to-day things might make a difference?

Rating
1—not even close to where you need and want to be
2—working on it but not effective
3—adequate
4—pretty effective
5—I'm good on this one

Do people know you care?

Loyal to people who are not present?	1 2 3 4 5
Gossip or make discounting statements about others?	1 2 3 4 5
Check in with people and then listen?	1 2 3 4 5
Open and great with feedback, complaints, and problems?	1 2 3 4 5
Have the right motives and interests?	1 2 3 4 5

Do people see your conversation as authentic, honest, and appropriate?

Ever exaggerate or overdramatize a situation?	1 2 3 4 5
Make flip remarks, use humor or language inappropriately?	1 2 3 4 5
Admit mistakes; apologize; say you are sorry?	1 2 3 4 5
Acknowledge other people's contributions, especially to yourself?	1 2 3 4 5
Listen in a nonjudgmental way?	1 2 3 4 5
Give people your undivided attention?	1 2 3 4 5
Disclose what you know, think, and believe?	1 2 3 4 5

Are your actions seen as consistent with your speaking?

Model what you say you value?	1 2 3 4 5
Keep confidences and treat conversations with respect?	1 2 3 4 5
Follow through with commitments, conversations, and people?	1 2 3 4 5
Do the right thing even though it's not fair?	1 2 3 4 5

Are you reliable?

Return phone calls promptly?	1 2 3 4 5
Stay caught up on e-mail?	1 2 3 4 5
Make and keep specific commitments?	1 2 3 4 5
Communicate when you can't deliver?	1 2 3 4 5
On time?	1 2 3 4 5
Accessible?	1 2 3 4 5

Do you deal with the rest of the world in a way that others respect?

Do you have an effective response to problems?	1 2 3 4 5
Do you have integrity?	1 2 3 4 5

Are you competent?

Are you organized? Have your act together?	1 2 3 4 5
Do you know your field?	1 2 3 4 5
Are you personally effective?	1 2 3 4 5
Do you run effective meetings?	1 2 3 4 5
Do you manage people well?	1 2 3 4 5

Group assessment: How good are we?

Where is the group with each of the following areas? Use the scale simply as the beginning of a conversation and exploration.

Rating
1—not even close to where you need and want to be
2—working on it but not effective
3—adequate
4—pretty effective
5—I'm good on this one

Everyone is excited, engaged, and aligned about the goals.	1 2 3 4 5
There is clarity about what working together makes possible.	1 2 3 4 5
There are clear, explicit agreements for working together of which everyone is aware.	1 2 3 4 5
A way has been established to make and keep commitments with each other.	1 2 3 4 5
An effective way is in place to surface and deal with problems.	1 2 3 4 5
There is a specific set of worthwhile goals and short-term milestones to create and maintain a sense of urgency.	1 2 3 4 5
There are ways to get to know each other so there is quick, effective communication.	1 2 3 4 5

Meetings are designed and managed in a
way that is highly productive.   1 2 3 4 5

Relationships and communications
within the group are sound.   1 2 3 4 5

Processes are in place for identifying and
managing key relationships outside the group.   1 2 3 4 5

Everyone is always working on building an
awareness and concern for the well-being
of others.   1 2 3 4 5

There is a willingness and ability to confront
everything that doesn't work.   1 2 3 4 5

Self-assessment: How effective am I?

Rating
1—not even close to where you need and want to be
2—working on it but not effective
3—adequate
4—pretty effective
5—I'm good on this one

Ability to design and manage conversations
- Design individual conversations for outcomes   1 2 3 4 5
- Keep conversations on track   1 2 3 4 5
- Encourage and support participation by everyone   1 2 3 4 5
- Bring conversations to appropriate closure   1 2 3 4 5

Ability to participate in a group setting effectively
- Clear sense of what I bring to a group   1 2 3 4 5
- Awareness of my conversational style and its impact 1 2 3 4 5
- Process skills and ability to notice what's needed   1 2 3 4 5
- Willingness to say what is so for me   1 2 3 4 5
- Clear about the leverage available in groups   1 2 3 4 5

Ability to influence others
- Act in a way that leads to trust and respect   1 2 3 4 5
- Am seen as supportive and helpful   1 2 3 4 5
- What I say makes a difference   1 2 3 4 5
- Appreciate what listening and understanding offer   1 2 3 4 5
- Value relationship building and find time to do it 1 2 3 4 5

Ability to perform
- Clear about my commitments and projects   1 2 3 4 5
- Able to create and maintain relationships   1 2 3 4 5
- Focused and attentive to the moment   1 2 3 4 5
- Operate with integrity   1 2 3 4 5
- Make and ask for clear commitments   1 2 3 4 5

Appendix D
Tools for Continued Exploration

This section provides checklists for reminding yourself about the ideas presented throughout the book and for sharpening your awareness of the variables to pay attention to as you work toward meeting mastery. These checklists can also be used when asking people to give you feedback.

Key relationship checklist

If you think about relationships as a pattern of conversations, you can reflect on your key relationships to get a sense of the quality of the relationship or where you might need to do some work. Reflect on the following questions, first from your point of view, then considering what other people would say if asked these questions about you.

Note that these questions are designed to look at the relationships that matter most to you—which means family and friends. Some questions will not be applicable when looking at a work relationship.

Are the conversations sufficient?

- Do we talk often enough?
- Are we talking about what I want to talk about?
- Am I willing to talk; to say what I am thinking?
- Am I willing to listen when they need to talk?
- Do recent conversations reflect the kind of relationship I want?

Do the relationships provide what I need?

- Do I feel acknowledged and appreciated?
- Do I feel listened to and understood?
- Are we having fun? Can we laugh together?
- Is there a future we are working on together?
- Do I feel supported?
- Are they available? Are they around enough?
- Is there caring and kindness present?
- Can I ask for what I want and need?

Do I admire and respect them?

- Do I respect the way in which they deal with the world?
- Do I have any limiting interpretations about them?
- Can I listen to them in a nonjudgmental way?
- Am I clear that they would be fine without me?
- Am I clearly on their side? Do they know it?
- Am I interested in their commitments and projects?

Is the relationship free of baggage?

- Do we talk about the relationship?
- Are we able to raise issues and complaints?
- Are we clear that problems are to be expected?
- Are we able to forgive what happened in the past and not have it taint the present or future?
- Can they make mistakes with me?

Summary: What do I need to pay attention to?

Conversational checklist for managers

Read through this checklist each day, and keep track of anything you notice throughout the day.

Are you aware of your impact on others?

- Whose productivity and well being do you impact?
- Do you consider the mood of the organization to be something you impact?
- Who are you mentoring, advising, teaching, or coaching?
- Are you providing an opportunity for people to converse in a meaningful way?

What conversations do people associate with you?

- Are the conversations that you are putting into the organization empowering or discounting?
- What questions are you asking of your people? What questions would make a difference?
- Are you providing clarity, focus, and future?

Are you authentic?

- Do you ever hold back things that you feel are important?
- Have you withheld feedback because you weren't certain the other person could handle it?
- Are you so indirect that people don't get what you are saying?
- Have you feigned modesty for something you are really proud of?
- Can you say what you are thinking in every setting?

What is it like to talk with you?

- Can you make the world stop when someone wants your attention?
- Are you great with people, even when you don't have time?
- Can you handle complaints and opposition in a great way?
- How do you react to problems? Is it empowering?
- Are you known for tact and diplomacy?

Do you speak and act with intention?

- Can you effectively manage meeting conversations?
- Can you notice what is missing in a conversation, meeting, or relationship and provide it?
- When you say you will do something, is it with every intention to deliver?
- Are your actions consistent with your speaking?
- What are you producing with your speaking?
- What are you producing with the way you listen?

Reflect on each of the sets of questions on the checklist and see if any strike you as especially relevant given your own experience. Then determine where you need to put some attention and focus. Here are some additional questions for reflection:

- What does the checklist make you aware of?
- What thinking can you add to this?
- What examples do you have?

Speaking checklist

It's nice to have a polished speaking style, but it is more important to be authentic and intentional about communicating. A colleague, Charles Graves, greatly influenced my work in this area. In the lists below, note your strengths and where you need to pay more attention:

Action does matter: We pay a price when we do not follow through on what we say we will do or we don't act consistent with what we say is important. Be a good role model.

Listen and be interested first: This isn't a rule. Speaking has more impact if we are known for our listening.

Tell people what you are thinking: We are all easier to work with if people do not have to guess about what we want or think.

Set up, set up, set up: Setting up a conversation at the beginning or setting up a question before asking it makes it easier to be heard.

Know your style: Each conversational style has strengths and weaknesses. Certain conversational preferences work best in business settings. Being clear, concise, straightforward, and responsible for what you are saying is the most powerful approach.

Watch your speaking: People are looking at the clarity of your speaking and making an assessment about your leadership ability or potential. You don't get to be unclear. You don't get to be tentative or vague.
- Resist speaking too quickly. Go slowly. Take your time.
- Going on and on can diminish your effectiveness.
- Speak up so you can easily be heard.
- Tone of voice is critical. Maintain the right tone.

- Use organizing techniques such as: *"I have three points to make…"*
- Try to make every sentence count.
- Don't discount your speaking in any way when you begin.
- Don't introduce extraneous thoughts or shift from one point to another.
- Speak concisely. Make your point in fifteen seconds. You can amplify after that if it makes sense.
- End on a strong note. Don't drop your voice with the last word of each sentence or thought.

Watch your words:

- Don't exaggerate. Let the facts speak.
- Don't make broad, sweeping generalizations.
- Don't use absolute language like *always* and *never*.
- Don't use thoughtless, trite expressions.
- Be selective in the use of nonspecific words such as *it, they, we*.
- Be sure each word contributes to the substance and spirit of the message.
- Be careful about humor that detracts from the conversation or participants.

Watch your nonverbal cues:

- Look at people for ten seconds as you begin speaking.
- Lean or step toward people when you listen.
- Be careful about nodding when you listen.
- Don't scowl or do anything that can be misinterpreted.
- Make sure your posture is attentive and supportive.

Influence practices checklist

Each of these individual practices creates or enhances your ability to influence others. Think about the ones you routinely use and choose three that would make a difference if you began to use them.

Encourage others to speak:

- Ask for ideas from others.
- Invite participation by everyone.
- Specifically ask people to speak or participate.

Be supportive when people participate:

- Help develop the ideas of others.
- Acknowledge what viewpoints people bring.
- Protect new and not-yet-feasible ideas.
- Allow people to finish their speaking.
- Avoid unsupportive nonverbal behavior.
- Listen generously and respond with tact.

Be easy to work with:

- Let others know they can disagree with you.
- Make your position power a nonissue.
- Be open to alternative approaches, ideas, and questions.
- Show interest in others as people.
- Be great with people after they disagree.
- React objectively when your ideas are challenged.
- Be thoughtful about how you say things.
- Present your ideas honestly.
- Be willing to be candid with people.
- Be accessible to people.
- Acknowledge when people have changed your thinking.

Manage the conversation process:

- Clarify conversations when needed.
- Ask questions to deepen the discussion.
- Simplify complex conversations.
- Summarize where the process is and suggest next steps.
- Keep the conversation on track.
- Stay out of the content if you are managing the process.
- Check out the process with the group before beginning.
- Capture and restate key points in the conversation.
- Summarize points of understanding.

Be responsible and reliable:

- Thoughtfully manage phone calls and e-mail each day.
- Give your word and keep it.
- Be specific in your requests and in your promises.
- Always include a "by when."
- Keep track of what you say you will do.
- Call when a promise is in jeopardy.
- Follow through and follow up.

Conversational moves to master

These statements and questions are designed to provide an effective way of responding to routine situations. Learn to identify these situations and practice using these responses.

- **Thank you. I appreciate being told.** It's important to acknowledge that you've heard someone's criticism or feedback without getting defensive or trying to explain your behavior. Acknowledging that you've heard what was said doesn't mean you are agreeing with it.

- **Here's what I'm taking away from our conversation.** This is one of the most powerful ways to acknowledge others—by letting them know what you value you received in being with them or from what they said. It also validates their contributions to the meeting or conversation. This is also very rare, so most people will appreciate it.

- **May I tell you something?** This not only secures permission, it prepares people to hear what you have to say, and it usually makes your tone of voice supportive—requesting rather than confronting.

- **Where are you with this?** Asking people what they are thinking or feeling about an issue gives them a chance to express whatever might be on their minds. This is a key conversational move in achieving alignment.

- **While I would have preferred a different approach, I'll fully support this.** It's easy to back an idea that matches your own preferences. Part of being an effective team member or family member is the ability to get behind ideas or decisions that are not your favorites.

- **This is what I appreciate about you.** People want to be liked; they want to have an impact. Letting them know what you like about them as a person is perhaps outside your comfort zone. Since people don't often express this kind of appreciation, it has an impact.

- **Tell me about…** Checking in with people about their experiences is a lost art. Doing so makes them feel included, valued, and appreciated. This phrase is also a way to ask people to say more in a conversation when you would like to hear more from them.

- **Did I answer your question?** It's easy to misinterpret someone's question. Or when you are trying to be concise, the question might not get fully answered. Asking this question is a simple, courteous way to ensure that your replies are effective.

- **Please say a bit more about what you are asking.** In addition to clarity, you will gain a better sense of the context for the question if you ask them to say more before you respond.

- **I have a request.** This lets people know that you are about to ask for something specific. It's a better option than hinting or asking indirectly, then being disappointed when you don't get what you want.

- **What is your request?** Behind every complaint is something people could ask for that would resolve the complaint. After listening fully, giving them a chance to "empty out" about their complaint. This question is the next step: asking them what would take care of their concern.

- **I'd be willing to do this for you.** Making a request is one way to create an action or a commitment. Making an offer is another way. Good team members and family members make offers to do things for others without being asked.

- **This is the value I see in what you are suggesting.** Rather than jumping into a conversation by saying that something won't work, try first looking for the value in an idea and then expressing your concern.

- **What else?** This is the equivalent of saying "Keep talking." Asking "Anything else?" is checking one last time for comments.

- **I'm not going to do anything with this. Is that OK?** People leave conversations expecting that you will do something simply because it was discussed. If you don't want this to happen, clarify what you will or will not do as you wrap up the conversation.

- **By when will you do that?** Asking for a specific commitment in time is an essential practice in project management. Any time you are concerned that something will not get done in a timely manner, make a point to nail down the "by when."

- **What would you like from me in this conversation?** Sometimes people come to you and begin discussing a topic without indicating what they are looking for in terms of your responses or in terms of outcomes. Consequently, it's difficult to know how to listen or participate. Asking them in the beginning will make the conversation more likely to turn out for both parties.

- **I think I'm clear about your idea, and I see it differently. May I tell you?** This is a way to set up your comments when you intend to disagree with what has been said. It both changes your tone of voice and makes it easier for them to hear your view. This phrase tends to take the right/wrong experience out of a conversation.

Checklist for managing projects and teams

You must find the balance between driving for results and taking great care of people. Somehow you must manage the reputation of the team and the project while not being stopped by worrying about what people think of you. And there are other things to consider—so many, in fact, that it is easy to become purely reactive instead of managing the project in a proactive way.

Therefore, it is important to find time each week to step back, create some distance, and look at the project from a different perspective. Consider these questions, share your thinking with others, and then do what makes sense to you.

How are your people doing?

- Are you routinely asking them?
- Is there a forum where they can ask questions, raise issues, and be listened to?
- Does anyone need support, resources, coaching?
- Is anyone feeling left out, overworked, unappreciated?
- Who needs to be acknowledged? Who would appreciate a note from you?
- Is everyone clear about the direction, outcomes, and current status of the project?
- Are they fully engaged? If not, what's in their way?
- Are they having fun? Who's in charge of fun? What's the next event?
- Are you managing people's development?
  - Are they getting the opportunities they expected to get?
  - Are you assigning work with an eye on development?
  - Are you taking time to train?
  - Are you debriefing successes and failures?
  - Do you know what people would like to try or learn?

How are people doing as a team?

- What is it going to take for this team to really start clicking?
- Are there any relationship issues? Are they being addressed?
- Do people know you won't tolerate relationship problems?
- Do people know one another well enough? If not, what can you do about it?
- Are the meetings which they conduct effective?
- Are people asking for help? Are they communicating problems?
- Are people looking out for each other?
- Does everyone own the entire project, or are there still turf issues?
- Are people doing whatever it takes to meet the commitments and milestones?

Is management on your side?

- Are they included, informed, and visible?
- Are they aware of how important they are to people?
- Where could they help? Do you have any requests for them?
- Is there anything you want them to know?
- Do you know what they want? Do they have complaints or concerns?
- What are they saying about the project to others?
- Do people clearly know that management is on their side?
- Are they inviting customers and clients to participate in the project?
- Do people feel connected to management and the organization? Has anything happened recently that might cause a disconnect?

How is the project going?

- Are we on target to produce the overall project outcomes? If not, what is missing?
- What is our current focus?
  - What is the next set of milestones?
  - Is anyone concerned or anxious about these next targets?

- - What's not moving? How do we get it moving?
  - Is there anything we haven't started yet that we need to address?
  - Are the accountabilities clear?
  - Do we have specific dates on every commitment?
- Are we measuring and tracking the right things?
- Are we working with a sense of urgency? Are we in a holding pattern anywhere?
- Does everyone associated with the project, including customers, management, and other parts of the organization, know how it is going? Are any of them anxious or concerned about anything?
- Do we have a sense of accomplishment about what we have achieved so far?
  - What have we produced since we began the project?
  - What is now possible that wasn't possible when we started?
  - What have we learned? What new thinking has emerged?
  - What problems have we handled? What breakthroughs have we had?
  - What should we feel really good about?

What can we do to take the project to a new level?

- If there were no alternative except to produce the result, what else would we be doing?
- Are we compromising anywhere on cost, schedule, or performance?
- Where can we gain time? If we had to take 25 percent off the schedule, how would we do it?
- Do we have the expertise we need? If we could get anybody, who would we ask for?
- Is it time to raise the stakes? Can we achieve more than we originally promised?
- How do we make it more fun and satisfying?
- How can we increase the learning and development?

Project team questions

- What has management asked us to produce?
  - What do we know is possible?
  - What do we think might be possible?
  - What are we willing to publicly commit to?
  - What are we willing to publicly "go for"?
- Is there anything that anyone is curious about, wondering about, anxious about, concerned about, or just wants to know? Any rumor you want to check out?
- Is everyone clear about the objectives and our path forward? Any new concerns about reaching the objectives?
- Is there anything in the way, or missing, that keeps us from being completely excited, engaged, and aligned?
- Is everything moving that needs to be moving? If not, what do we do? Are we on the path to produce the project and the results we want? If not, what is missing?
- Do we have the next set of short-term milestones in front of everyone? Do they create the sense of urgency we need?
- What do we need to be paying attention to and managing right now? Is there anything that we are not addressing or that we are overlooking?
- Is there anything in our way? Individually? As a team? As a project?
- Does anyone know of any problems or potential problems that we have not brought to the surface or addressed? Are we responding in a way that has people raise problems, issues, and concerns? Do people know how to get problems handled?
- Who needs to be acknowledged?
  - Who needs to know that we value and appreciate them?
  - Who needs to be included?

- Is everyone OK? Anyone need time off? Anyone need support?
- How is our relationship with our sponsors? Stakeholders? Key managers?
- What external relationships are important?
  - Are they sufficient?
  - Who is accountable for, and managing, each?
- Do we have any workability issues?
  - Any breaks in relationship or communication?
  - Any disagreements, misunderstandings, or complaints?
  - Do we have the agreements in place to ensure ongoing workability?
  - Are we using "X by Y" and delivering?
- Are our communications inside and outside the project sufficient?
- Is the reputation of the project where we want it?
- Can we go "flat out" if we need to? Do we need to go "flat out" in any area?
- Would more resources help us anywhere?
- What else could we do to get more leverage?
- Are we developing people as we go?
  - Do the project members feel they are in development?
- Are we having fun? Who is in charge of fun?
- What have we accomplished?
  - What have we produced, learned, made possible?
- Is there anything else we need to do in order to be complete with this project?
- What are the conversations we need to have together?

How can we ensure that this won't fall apart later?

Often projects get off to a good start, only to break down or slowly erode over time. If you haven't experienced this at work, you may have in your personal life. Think of a time when you started a project (exercising, remodeling, spending more time with your kids) only to notice a month later that progress had slowed or you were no longer working on it. In situations like this, the tendency seems to be to blame a lack of commitment. Not so. It's more likely you didn't set up the necessary structures, supports, and systems to keep things going. When you begin your next project, spend time considering what you need to put in place to ensure this project won't break down.

What structures do we need to put in place?
- What are our key targets and milestones?
- What reviews do we need and with whom?
- Do we need to schedule ongoing meetings, calls, or conversations?

What systems would be helpful?
- What are we going to record, measure, and track?
- Who will keep track of all of our promises and requests?

What relationships do we need in order to be successful?
- Who do we need to involve or consult with?
- Do we need a management sponsor?
- Who will we talk to when we run into problems?
- Is this a time when we should utilize coaching?
- What other support might we need? From whom?

What agreements do we need to make with each other?
- Are we going to do what we say or call?
- Are we going to raise issues and concerns as they arise?

> *"Everyone who has taken a shower has had an idea.*
> *It's the person who gets out of the shower, dries off, and*
> *does something about it who makes a difference."*
>
> —Nolan Bushnell, Founder of Atari

Meeting Roles

The Provost Council at a Land Grant University I've worked with developed a definition of meeting roles that breaks down something like this:

Owner

Typically, this is the person who asked to put a topic on the agenda. The owner sets up this conversation for the group, which might include:

- Framing the topic in a longer time frame or process (context)
- Setting outcomes for today
- Explaining what the owner is looking for from meeting members
- Establishing time and process, if process is complex

With straightforward and short-duration discussions, the owner is also usually the person who manages the group conversation.

Whether leading or not, the owner is also responsible for looking for the value that occurs during the conversation and providing closure at the end of the conversation.

Leader

On complex or longer conversations, it's useful to have someone who can manage the group conversation without adding content.

Responsibilities include working with the owner to set up, check progress, and close the conversation.

This person is also responsible for making sure that the process for working through the conversation is clear and then keeping the conversation on track.

The leader manages the levels of conversation so everyone feels heard and included.

This person either provides a charting of the conversation or asks someone else to do so.

The leader asks someone to keep track of the conversation so pertinent points can be captured in the minutes of the meeting.

Meeting Participants

In addition to participating in the conversation, participants look for ways to help the owner and the leader to both accomplish the work on each topic and ensure that everyone has a good experience of being in the meeting.

Those with less content to provide on a topic can pay more attention to process and provide guidance on where the conversation is and where it might go next.

Observing meetings

These are things to watch for when you are asked to observe a meeting.

Before the meeting:

- Have the right people been invited?
- Was the agenda sent out in advance so participants could prepare?
- Is the number of agenda items appropriate to the time available?

Setup:

- Were the participants asked if the agenda was clear?
- Were they asked if there were other topics to add to the agenda?
- Was it clear there was permission to manage the meeting?
- Were agreements or meeting practices reviewed?

Discussion management:

- Was each agenda item introduced with outcomes, times, and clear process steps?
- Was the conversation kept on track but with freedom for back-and-forth discussion?
- Was clarity evident? Did participants speak candidly?
- Was each conversation taken to completion with agreement on next steps and specific commitments?

Levels of participation:

- Were people invited into the conversation when appropriate?
- Overall, did there seem to be a balance in participation?
- When someone spoke, did he or she have the group's attention?
- Did each person's speaking seem honored and treated as valuable?

Try This

This checklist combines all of the action items throughout the book in one place. A printable list is available at paulaxtell.com.

Strategy 1: Choose the Perspective: This Matters

☐ Practice doing one thing at a time. Focus all of your attention on this particular situation in this moment. See what happens.

☐ Catch yourself not looking forward to something, then find a new perspective.

☐ Practice owning the meetings you attend, then be aware of what you notice and what you might do differently.

☐ Put together a collection of seven phrases that remind you of how you want to deal with life.

Strategy 2: Master Effective Conversation

☐ For the next week, stop and devote your full attention to everyone who speaks to you.

☐ Allow people to finish without interruption.

☐ Be slower to offer solutions or advice.

☐ In your meetings for the next week, observe conversations for clarity.

☐ Whenever you notice yourself wondering what someone else means, ask for clarity.

☐ After each meeting, reflect on what you said and how you said it, taking note of your observations or insights.

☐ As each meeting topic is wrapped up, assess it against the four elements of effective conversation: clarity, candor, commitment, and completion. Speak up if anything is missing that would be useful to add.

☐ Look for examples of how words shape the world for you and others.

Strategy 3: Create Supportive Relationships

☐ Listen for what you can learn about people in each meeting.

☐ Notice the response of others when you are intentional about connecting with them.

☐ Leave each meeting with the name of someone with whom to follow up.

☐ Observe how other people open conversations. How do the people who excel at working the room begin their conversations with you? How do senior people interact with others in meetings?

☐ Develop a set of conversation openers that resonate with you. Here's a starter set:

- *I'd love to hear about your career. Tell me about your early days with the organization.*

- *Tell me about your family.*

- *What are your outside interests?*

- *What projects are you working on?*

- *Do you have any interesting trips planned for this year?*

Be willing to ask simple questions: *I have no idea what you do—can you explain that to me?*

☐ Encourage people to tell you more about themselves.

☐ Notice when people want you to talk.

☐ Invite someone to coffee.

☐ Listen in a way that honors each person who speaks. Devote yourself to each of the conversations in which you participate. Hold back your questions and just listen. Use the phrase, *"Tell me more."* Stay silent when people finish a thought to see if they start speaking again.

☐ Recover the lost art of checking in with people. Ask people about their interests, their projects, their travels, their kids. It doesn't take much time. Ask a question, and then listen for three or four minutes.

☐ Learn to work the room. For many people, working the room and interacting with others in a wonderful, gracious way does not come naturally. That's fine, but it doesn't excuse you from getting good at this if you work in an organization.

☐ Keep track of your relationships. Maintaining a journal of people you meet and your conversations with them will help you remember.

☐ Reconnect with two people each week.

Strategy 4: Decide What Matters and Who Cares

☐ For every meeting, list the possibilities and value associated with each topic on the agenda.

☐ Make a list of what matters to your group or organization and compare it to your agenda topics for the last three weeks.

☐ Give people permission to question whether their attendance is required.

Strategy 5: Design Each Conversation

☐ For two weeks, listen for the setup on every topic and assess whether it was adequate.

☐ For two weeks, listen for the elements of closure and assess whether the wrap-up for each topic was adequate.

☐ Set aside fifteen minutes to prepare for each of your next five one-on-one meetings and see if you notice a qualitative difference in how they work.

Strategy 6: Lead Meetings for Three Outcomes

☐ Focus on critical variables for the setup:

- Have you established permission to lead and agreements for the group? Do people know they can say or ask anything?
- Are the outcomes for each conversation clear?
- Is the process to be followed clear?

☐ Focus on critical variables for managing the conversation:
- Has the conversation veered off track?
- Has each conversation been taken to completion with next steps identified?
- Was everyone taken care of during the conversation?

Strategy 7: Participate in Meetings to Have Impact

☐ Listen for what others are interested in or care about.

☐ Listen for the value being created in the conversation.

☐ Listen for what each person is dealing with in his or her area.

☐ Listen for what you appreciate about each person.

☐ Listen for opportunities to contribute to the conversation.

☐ Notice when you have an idea to share but don't speak.

☐ Rate your speaking for how clear, concise, relevant, and respectful it was.

☐ After each meeting for the next two weeks, reflect on what you said, how you said it, and what impact your comments had on the group conversation.

☐ Reflect on what you bring to a particular meeting or group:
- *What do people rely on you for?*
- *What do they appreciate about their interactions with you?*

☐ Begin to observe people who speak in a way you admire. What is it about what they say or how they say it that elicits respect?

Strategy 8: Build Remarkable Groups

☐ Notice what you say outside of the meeting about the group or individuals in the group. If it is not positive, learn to keep from saying it.

☐ Look for what you might offer in terms of support to other team members.

- ☐ Invite the newest member of the team to coffee and see if he or she would like support.
- ☐ Think about how you might ask the group to support you.

The Art of Learning

- ☐ Choose a learning perspective for meetings—go into each one prepared to observe and learn as much as you can about what makes them successful.
- ☐ When you are around small children, watch them learn and remind yourself what it's like to be open and curious and fine with not knowing all the answers.
- ☐ Use each meeting as an opportunity to develop meeting mastery. In every meeting for a series of about ten, pick something to look for from the lists above. Notice what you notice and make notes. Then pick something else for the next ten meetings, and so on.
- ☐ Notice what there is to notice on your drive to work. This will give you practice with the idea of observing and seeing what there is to see. This is the first step in being mindful.
- ☐ Go into a meeting with the self-instruction to just hear and see what is there to be heard and seen.
- ☐ Each day find fifteen to twenty minutes to reflect on an important conversation.
- ☐ Don't put the car radio on while driving or the earbuds in while running or cycling and notice where your mind goes.
- ☐ After every meeting, take a moment and note what you learned.
- ☐ After important meetings, schedule forty-five minutes to debrief with someone, perhaps over lunch or on a walk. Use these questions: *What did you notice during the meeting? What insights do you have? What are you now thinking about? What might you have done differently?*

☐ If any of your employees are working on meeting skills, provide support by debriefing with them once or twice a month over coffee.

☐ Read a section or chapter of this book for fifteen minutes, twice a week, and then relax and wait for the insights and connections to appear as you attend meetings.

☐ In meetings, split your note-taking paper into two sections. Use the left-hand two-thirds for notes on the topics that are discussed. Use the right-hand third of the page to record your insights about the meeting process.

☐ Don't allow yourself to do other work in a meeting or take anything into the meeting that might distract you.

☐ Keep side conversations to a minimum.

☐ Create three blocks of time each week for uninterrupted work.

☐ Replace the "smart" technology gadget that connects you with (and pulls you into) the world outside the meeting with a small paper notebook to record your insights. Notice the difference in your focus and participation—and the quality of your insights.

☐ Ask someone to observe as you lead a meeting or when you're presenting during a meeting.

☐ Begin keeping a journal of daily insights.

Guidelines for Managers

☐ Find a way to remind yourself that you matter to others.

☐ Slow down and acknowledge people you meet.

☐ Ask people for input (*What do you think?*) and where they stand on issues (*Where are you with this?*).

☐ For the next week, acknowledge a presenter in every meeting by sharing what you are taking away from his or her remarks.

"The composer Stravinsky had written a new piece with a difficult violin passage. After it had been in rehearsal for several weeks, the solo violinist came to Stravinsky and said he was sorry, he had tried his best, the passage was too difficult, no violinist could play it. Stravinsky said, 'I understand that. What I am after is the sound of someone trying to play it.'"

—Thomas Powers
American author

Bibliography

Each of the following articles and books influenced my thinking in developing the strategies for making meetings more effective. They provide opportunities to delve more deeply into the concepts presented in this book, and I recommend them to you.

Allison, Elle, and Douglas B. Reeves. *Renewal Coaching: Sustainable Change for Individuals and Organizations.* San Francisco: Jossey-Bass, 2009.

Brown, Judy. "Dialogue: Capacities and Stories," chapter in *Learning Organizations: Developing Cultures for Tomorrow's Workplace.* Sarita Chawla and John Renesch, eds. Portland, OR: Productivity Press, 2006.

Carnegie, Dale. *How to Win Friends and Influence People.* New York: Simon & Schuster, 2009 (reissue edition; originally published in 1937).

Colvin, Geoff. *Talent Is Overrated: What Really Separates World-Class Performers from Everybody Else.* New York: Portfolio Trade, 2010.

Csikszentmihalyi, Mihaly. *Good Business: Leadership, Flow, and the Making of Meaning.* New York: Penguin Books, 2004.

de Mello, Anthony. *Awareness.* New York: Random House, 2011.

Drucker, Peter. "My Life as a Knowledge Worker," *Inc.,* February 1, 1997.

Duarte, Nancy. *Resonate: Present Visual Stories That Transform Audiences.* New Jersey: Wiley, 2010.

Ellinor, Linda, and Glenna Gerard. *Dialogue: Rediscover the Transforming Power of Conversation.* New Jersey: Wiley, 1998.

Fine, Debra. *The Fine Art of Small Talk: How to Start a Conversation, Keep It Going, Build Networking Skills--and Leave a Positive Impression!* New York: Hyperion, 2005.

Gallwey, Timothy W. *The Inner Game of Work: Focus, Learning, Pleasure, and Mobility in the Workplace.* New York: Random House, 2001.

Gladwell, Malcolm. *Blink: The Power of Thinking Without Thinking.* New York: Little Brown, 2005.

Harkins, Phil. *Powerful Conversations.* New York: McGraw-Hill, 2001.

Heifetz, Ronald. *Leadership Without Easy Answers.* Cambridge: Harvard University Press, 1998.

Herjavec, Robert. *Driven: How to Succeed in Business and in Life.* New York: HarperCollins, 2010.

Horowitz, Seth. *The Universal Sense: How Hearing Shapes the Mind.* New York: Bloomsbury, 2012.

Jackson, Maggie. *Distracted: The Erosion of Attention and the Coming Dark Age.* New York: Prometheus, 2009.

Jaworski, Joseph. *Synchronicity: The Inner Path of Leadership.* San Francisco: Berrett-Koehler Publishers, 2011.

King, Larry. *How to Talk to Anyone, Anytime, Anywhere: The Secrets of Good Communication.* New York: Three Rivers Press, 2007.

Lamott, Anne. *Bird by Bird: Some Instructions on Writing and Life.* New York: Anchor Books, 1995.

Nerburn, Kent. *Letters to My Son: A Father's Wisdom on Manhood, Life, and Love.* 2nd edition. New York: New World Library, 1999.

Nichols, Michael P. *The Lost Art of Listening.* New York: Guilford Press, 1995.

Palmer, Parker. *The Courage to Teach: Exploring the Inner Landscape of a Teacher's Life.* San Francisco: Jossey-Bass, 1997.

Rosen, Christine, "The Myth of Multitasking," *The New Atlantis*, Number 20, Spring 2008: 105–110.

Rotella, Bob. *Golf is Not a Game of Perfect*. New York: Simon & Schuster, 2007.

Sandra, Jaida n'ha. *Salons: The Joy of Conversation*. British Columbia: New Society Publishers, 2001.

Scott, Susan. *Fierce Conversations: Achieving Success at Work and in Life One Conversation at a Time*. New York: Berkley Books, 2004.

Shafir, Rebecca Z. *The Zen of Listening: Mindful Communication in the Age of Distraction*. Adyar, Madras, India: Quest Books, 2012.

Schein, Edgar H. *Process Consultation Revisited: Building the Helping Relationship*. Boston: Addison Wesley Longman, 1998.

Sull, Donald N., and Charles Spinosa. "Promise-Based Management," *Harvard Business Review*, April 2007.

Tannen, Deborah. *You Just Don't Understand: Women and Men in Conversation*. New York: Harper Paperbacks, 2001.

Ueland, Brenda. "Tell Me More," *Utne Reader*, November–December 1992; excerpted from *Strength to Your Sword Arm: Selected Writings*. Duluth, MN: Holy Cow Press, 1993.

Wheatley, Margaret J. *Leadership and the New Science: Discovering Order in a Chaotic World*. Oakland, CA: Berrett-Koehler Publishers, 2006.

Wycoff, Joyce. *Mindmapping: Your Personal Guide to Exploring Creativity and Problem-Solving*. New York: Berkley Trade, 1991.

Index

Adams, Scott, xvii, 61

agenda setting and accomplishment, 69–76, 90–92. *See also* leadership

alignment, creation of, 108–110, 135–136, 157–158

Allison, Elle, 60

appreciation, expression of, 137–138, 283–284

asking for what you need, 185–187

assessment tools
    for conversations, 312–313
    external relationships, 302–303
    group assessment, 306–307
    for influence practices, 316–317
    project management, 321–323
    project team assessment, 324–326
    for relationships, 310–311
    self-assessment, 308
    for speaking, 314–315
    trust and respect, 304–306

attendance at meetings, 76–81

attentiveness, 59–64, 170. *See also* listening; mindfulness

attitude, 16, 20

authenticity, 56–57, 77–78, 163

awareness, 216–217. *See also* mindfulness

beginning new projects, 104–105

Berra, Yogi, 217

Bird by Bird (Lamott, Anne), 10, 223

Brown, Judy, 7, 172–173

candor in conversation, 32–33, 35–36

caring, 29

Carson, Johnny, 180

chance encounters, 239–241

checking in, 59–61, 280

civility, 36

clarity in conversation, 32–35, 175–176, 253

closure, 93–94, 97, 111–112, 134–139

coffee with coworkers, 46–47, 59

collective wisdom, 7

commitment in conversation, 32–33, 37–38, 136, 187, 271–272

compassion, 59

complaints, 255–258

concensus, 108–110

confidentiality, 241

conversations. *See also* listening
    assessment of, 312–313
    attentiveness and, 59–64, 170
    candor and, 32–33, 35–36
    clarity and, 32–35, 175–176, 253
    closure, 93–94, 97, 111–112, 134–139
    commitment and, 32–33, 37–38, 136, 187, 271–272
    completion and, 32–33, 38
    design of, 9, 83–92, 112–115
    difficult, 272–275
    effectiveness of, 8, 25–26
    importance of, 5–6, 38–40
    meetings as, 83–87
    moves to master, 318–320
    networking and, 51–59
    process steps, 93–94, 97–110, 129–132, 288–289
    relationships and, 48–51
    setup, 90, 93–96, 128–129
    speaking style and, 31–32

coworkers, 46–47, 59

cultural differences, 146, 149–150

daily start-up meetings, 279

deadlines, 37

debriefing, 219–220

decision making, 97, 106–107
delegating leadership, 242–246
disagreements, 180–181, 258
distractions, 127, 171–172, 224–226.
    See also mindfulness

Eiseley, Loren, 169
Eldridge, Emerson, 233
employee Q&A sessions, 246–254
engaging people, 236–239
Evans, Gwil, 138, 287
external relationships, 302–303

familiarity, 46–57, 199–201
feedback, 226–229, 245, 285–287
follow up, 139–142
friendships, professional, 50–51, 58
front-end loading, 221–222

Gerstner, Louis, 131
getting to know people, 46–57
goals/goal-setting, 198, 278
Golf Is Not a Game of Perfect (Rotella),
    71–72
gossip, 204–207
greetings, 53
group attendance, 76–81, 92
groups
    assessment of, 306–307
    check-in, 59–61, 280
    conversation and, 48–49
    familiarity and, 9, 199–201
    guidelines for, 201–203
    importance of, 193–197
    leverage and momentum and, 6–7
    productivity and, 208–209
    respect and, 206–207
    responsibility and, 204–205
    sense of purpose and, 197–198

group size, 35, 77–78, 92, 114–115
guest speakers, 248

Haeffele, Lynn, 142–144, 146
Holland, Dave, 199
humor, 180

inappropriate comments, 269–271
inclusion, 235
ineffective behaviors. *See* negative
    behaviors/mindsets
influence practices, 316–317
input requests, 97, 100–101, 281–282
intentions, 21, 36, 52, 266–267
interruptions, 268
introductions, 52

Johnson, Rob, 15
journaling, 223–224

Lamott, Anne, 10, 223
leading
    agreements for, 125–128
    authenticity and, 163
    closure and, 134–139
    cultural differences and, 149–150
    delegating of, 242–246
    follow up, 139–142
    importance of, 121–122
    influence practices, 316–317
    key variables, 215
    mindfulness and, 162
    objectives of, 123
    participation and, 151–159, 182–183
    permission of group for, 124
    setup for, 128–129
    skill development and, 159–162
    staying on track, 129–134
    virtual meetings and, 142–148

learning
    ability for, 213–214
    debriefing and, 219–220
    distractions and, 224–226
    feedback and, 226–229
    front-end loading and, 221–222
    importance of, 9
    journaling and, 223–224
    key variables, 214–216
    mindfulness and, 217
    reflection and, 218–219
Lincoln, Abraham, 47
listening, 26–30, 48–49, 53, 169–174,
    238–239, 292–295. *See also*
    attentiveness; conversations
The Lost Art of Listening (Nichols), 28

managers, guidelines for
    chance encounters and, 239–241
    complaints and, 255–258
    conversation assessment, 312–313
    delegating leadership, 242–246
    employee Q&A sessions, 246–254
    engaging people, 236–237
    inclusion and, 235
    listening, 238–239
    overview, 9–10
    people matter, 233–234
    project assessment checklist,
        321–323
    project team assessment, 324–326
mediocrity, 15–16
meeting new people, 55–57
meeting roles, 325–326
meeting summary, 132, 141, 183, 208
mindfulness, 17–19, 162, 217. *See also*
    distractions
mind mapping, 132–133
mindset, 8, 15–21

minutes, 141–142. *See also* meeting
    summary
multitasking, 171–172, 224–226
names, using, 53–54
Nass, Clifford, 171
needs being met, 185–187
negative behaviors/mindsets
    benefit of the doubt and, 266–267
    broken commitments, 271–272
    difficult conversations, 272–275
    inappropriate comments, 269–271
    interruptions, 268
    options for responding, 267–268
    overview, 263–265
    perspectives on meetings and, 19–20
    talking too much, 269
Nelson, Byron, 71–72
Nerburn, Kent, 206
networking, 8, 51–59
Nichols, Michael, 28
nonjudgmental participation, 173–174

observing meetings, 329
one-on-one meetings, 113–114
outcome enhancement, 9
outcomes desired, 90, 93–96
outsiders, 81

participating
    asking for what you need, 185–187
    key variables, 215
    leadership and, 151–159
    listening and, 169–174
    other participants and, 183–185
    ownership and, 9, 167–169
    self-awareness and, 188–189
    speaking and, 175–182
    support for leader and, 182–183
patience, 172–173

performance review, 283–284
personal sharing, 53, 58, 76
perspectives
    empowering choices, 8, 15–21
    participation and, 167–169
Peters, Tom, 45, 63
photo sharing, 299
point of view, 8, 15–21
Power Point, 131
problem solving, 97, 102–103
process steps, 86, 93–94, 97–110,
    129–132, 288–289
productivity, 208–209
progress reports, 97–99
project management. *See* management
    guidelines
purpose, sense of, 197–198

Q&A sessions, 246–254

reflection, 218–219
relationships
    assessment of, 310–311
    attention and, 59–64
    conversation and, 48–49
    external, 302–303
    familiarity and, 199–200
    importance of, 45–46
    keeping track of, 54, 62–63
    networking and, 51–59
relationship-building exercises,
    291–299
    at work, 47–51
Renewal Coaching (Allison), 60
respect, 206–207, 304–306
respectful speaking, 179
Rilke, Rainer Maria, 204
Rogers, Carl, 29, 173
Roper, Larry, 7, 39–40, 149

Rotella, Bob, 71–72
roundtable discussions, 287
Ruiz, Don Miguel, 125

Schein, Edgar H., 110
Scheuermann, Tom, 50–51
self-assessment, 308, 324
self-awareness, 188–189
Senge, Peter, 108
sense of purpose, 197–198
speaking skills, 175–182, 269, 314–315
speaking style, 31–32
staff meetings, 75
starting new projects, 97, 104–105
start-up meetings, daily, 279
staying on track, 129–134, 186
Stevens, Michael, 180
Sullivan, Ed, 59
supervisor interview, 297–298
Sutton, Robert, 77

time investments, 54, 70–72, 90–91
tracking relationships, 61–64
trust, 46, 197, 199–201, 250, 304–306

Ueland, Brenda, 27
using people's names, 53–54

virtual meetings, 85–86, 116–117,
    142–148
visual aids, 131

Wainwright, Adam, 15–16, 214
Watson, Thomas, 201
Wheatley, Margaret, 69
Whitfield School, 201
working the room, 52–55
X by Y, 37, 93–94, 136, 202, 325

Index of quotes

Abdul, Paula, 118
Andreas, Brian , xiv, 197, 259
Angelou, Maya, 20, 234
Astaire, Fred, 3
Bateson, Gregory, 31
Begeman, Michael, 84
Bohm, David, 6, 173
Bushnell, Nolan, 326
Cantu, Carlos, 246
Carey, Hugh, 300
Carnegie, Dale, 65
Csikszentmihalyi, Mihaly, xvii
Deming, W. Edwards, 169
DeVault, R. David, 251
Dillard, Annie, 66
Freud, Sigmund, 33
Gallwey, Tim, 175, 216, 219, 260
Garcia, Paul, 238
Gilligan, Carol, 35
Goleman, Daniel Jay, 217
Halberstam, David, 209
Hallowell, Edward M., 290
Hayes, Ainsley, 205
Hills, Jodi, 17
Holmes, Oliver Wendell, 223
Hughes, Dave, 199
James, William, 14
Jobs, Steve, 82
Lao-Tsu, 120
Leonard, George, 210
Lincoln, Abraham, 229å
Lombardi, Vince, 190

Maister, David, 226
McKibben, Bill, 224
Mead, Margaret, 68
Mother Teresa, 139
Mulcahy, Anne M., 254
Nimmer, Amy, xviii
Ogens, Eva, 224
Parkinson, C. Northcote, 91
Palmer, Parker, 163
Powers, Thomas, 336
Proust, Marcel, 12
Rilke, Rainer Maria, 204
Roper, Claudette, 40
Rosen, Christine, 226
Roosevelt, Eleanor, 262
Rowling, J.K., 164
Sandra, Jaida n'ha, 189, 203
Scott, Susan, 24, 41, 57, 230
Seneca, 49
Simon, Herbert, 276
Stafford, Rachel Macy, 239
Summitt, Pat, 192
Szasz, Thomas, 213
Tannen, Deborah, 22
Tutu, Desmond, 38
vos Savant, Marilyn, 171
Walsch, Neale Donald, 212
Webber, Alan, 232
Werner, Kenny, 162
Wheatley , Margaret J., 42, 218
Whyte, David, 44
Wilde, Oscar, 163
Wooden, John, 180

About the Author

Paul Axtell provides consulting and personal effectiveness training to a wide variety of clients, from Fortune 500 companies and universities to nonprofit organizations and government agencies. A large focus of his work is how to run effective and productive meetings—to turn them from the calendar items people dread into useful, productive sessions with measurable results.

Paul has an engineering degree from South Dakota School of Mines and an MBA from Washington University in St. Louis. He has ten years of engineering and manufacturing experience and fifteen years of experience in corporate personnel and training. The last twenty years have been devoted to designing and leading programs that enhance individual and group performance within large organizations.

He is the author of *Ten Powerful Things to Say to Your Kids: Creating the Relationship You Want with the Most Important People in Your Life*, which applies the concepts of his work to the special relationships between parents and children of all ages. Thus far, it has been translated into Korean, Vietnamese, Chinese, Arabic, French, and Spanish.

He is also the author of *Being Remarkable*, a small but power-er-packed collection of action items—gleaned from more than thirty years of coaching people toward greater personal effectiveness—aimed at developing the awareness that is the beginning of true and lasting change.

In addition to interacting with kids, he loves playing golf, creating bonsai trees, fly-fishing, and reading mysteries. Paul lives with his wife, Cindy, in Minneapolis.

Praise for Paul Axtell's
Ten Powerful Things to Say to Your Kids:
Creating the Relationship You Want
with the Most Important People in Your Life

"Words are powerful, so choosing them wisely is critical, especially when talking with our children. This book has great advice about what to say, and what not to say, to impressionable kids. Paul Axtell reminds us of the power of words to change lives, and about the fine art of listening. He encourages us to read together, play together, and grow together, unafraid of the mistakes we'll make along the way. If you yearn for a happier home, and meaningful conversations with more substantial answers than 'okay,' 'fine' and 'whatever,' this book is great place to start."

— Jim Barnes, Editor, IndependentPublisher.com
(Gold Medal winner: IPPY Award for Best Parenting Book of 2012)

"Parents struggle endlessly to maintain positive, effective relationships with their children. This book's insights come in bite-size nuggets that will stay with readers for far longer than the fleeting time it will take to read, but they contain potent tools for improving relationships with children of every age."

— Elizabeth Breau, *ForeWord Reviews*

"Axtell's advice is obvious in that it makes sense as soon as you read it. Yet, let's face it, the obvious is easy to forget in the crazy, frantic rush of the day.... Every chapter is a gem...."

— Naomi Karten, speaker and author of
Communication Gaps and How to Close Them

What you will read about in this book are things you can say to your kid today, right this moment. *Ten Powerful Things* not only creates great relationships with kids, it will create great kids.

—Elle Allison, author of *What Wise People Do* and *Renewal Coaching*